TOTUS TUUS MARIA

Contents

Introduction

By CAMERON FRADD

Hurt. Betrayed. Confused. Angry. This is how many women feel when they first discover their husband has been looking at pornography. When my husband, Matt, confessed to me during the second year of our marriage that he had been falling to pornography, I felt a whole slew of emotions that, even now, aren't easy to untangle. Searing disappointment. I remember feeling that. I thought porn was something that only creepy men struggled with, or men who had bad relationships with their wives, or who didn't find their wives attractive. And then it hit me like a sick joke.

Wait, does he not find me attractive? Is it the baby fat I haven't lost? If he's keeping this a secret from me, what else might he be hiding? He's been lying to me. How can I ever trust him again?

It would be one thing if I had discovered that he'd been throwing away the meals I'd been making him and then sneaking out to McDonald's. That would hurt, but this killed. He wasn't rejecting what I had made for him, or the ways I'd sought to show him love, he was rejecting *me*.

Those were lonely days. And, at that point, I knew no other women whose husbands struggled with porn. Well, that may not be true. It's more likely that I did know them, but they, like me, didn't talk about it. And that silence made the isolation all the greater.

This book exists to break the silence.

Both Matt (who, by God's grace, has experienced great freedom from pornography and masturbation) and I believe that wives are the forgotten victims in the carnage that porn addiction is wreaking in our society. I'm so thankful that many people are speaking out about the damage porn causes, and I've also been delighted to see a growing number of brave women speaking out about the reality of their own porn addiction and offering to help other women out of the mess they were once in. But who's addressing us wives? Who's taking *our* pain seriously?

According to authors Barbara Steffens and Marsha Means, 70 percent of wives dealing with spousal betrayal fit the criteria for PTSD. That's right, Post Traumatic Stress Disorder. Steffens explains, "Once disclosure happens, and her world is shattered, she is still expected to be wife, mother, she's working, a professional person, on the job. You don't get time off for this. We are lucky in our society to get three days off if we're grieving the loss of a loved one. We get no time off when our lives have been shattered due to sex addiction and this kind of betrayal."[1]

This book contains powerful stories from women who have experienced this pain, and have found, by God's grace, restoration. Peace. Healing. Even joy. These women are no different from you or me. They're not uber-holy, perfect women (though some come close), but, as you'll soon discover, they found comfort and strength in a holy and perfect God.

There is a beautiful scene in the film *Good Will Hunting* where Sean, a therapist, tells Will, a brilliant but angry young man, that all of the abuse and mistreatment he had experienced earlier in life wasn't his fault.

1. http://wyso.org/post/ptsd-partners-sex-addicts-0

Sean: It's not your fault.
Will: Yeah, I know that.
Sean: Look at me, son. It's not your fault.
Will: I know.
Sean: No. It's not your fault.
Will: I know
Sean: No, no, you don't. It's not your fault.
[Sean moves closer to Will]
Sean: Hmm?
Will: I know.
[Will stands up and distances himself from Sean]
Sean: It's not your fault.
Will: All right.
Sean: It's not your fault.

If I could leave you with one word of wisdom before you embark upon this book, it would be just that. *It's not your fault.* And you may think you know that already. But, like Will, you probably don't know it to the degree you need to. So listen to me, sister in Christ. It's not your fault.

It's not your fault that you aren't hundreds of two-dimensional Internet women. It's not your fault that you don't become sexually euphoric at the drop of a hat like the women in porn. It's not your fault that you aren't clickable and customizable. You are a woman. You are beautiful. You are God's daughter. And he, like any good father, wants good for you. Pause a moment and, if you're open to it, pray this prayer.

Lord, you are not unfamiliar with my grief. You know me through and through. You love to heal your children and I, your daughter, am in need of your healing, in need of you. I open my heart to you. Give me the grace to forgive those who have hurt me.

Especially _____. *Help me to take my identity first and foremost in being your beloved child.*

Jesus I trust in you, Jesus I trust in you, Jesus I trust in you. Hail Mary . . .

Restored

Confessions of a Redeemed Heart

By ELISA

If there's one myth I've heard repeated over and over again, it's that marriage will cure a man's desire for pornography. This— as you may already know too well—is false. Elisa began buying into the lie that she was somehow to blame for her husband looking at porn. I know many wives who think this way. They think, "If only I was prettier, bustier, more adventurous in bed, if I wasn't so critical, or if I [fill in the blank], he wouldn't turn to porn." But this, too, is false, and it's imperative to realize that. Listen, you can't cure a porn addict by giving him more sex for the same reason you can't cure a gambling addict by giving him more money. In both instances the addict is seeking not money or an orgasm, but the rush, the high, the thrill of the chase. The porn addict has trained himself to believe that sex should be something on-tap and made-to-order. He has bought into Burger King sex: he prefers it his way, right away. The problem is with him, not his wife.

—MATT

I fell in love with the man I married when we square-danced together as children. I was nine; he was fourteen and the most beautiful boy I had ever seen. What I felt was not the physically driven love of teenage years but the innocent, starry-eyed love of childhood. He was beautiful and funny, and I adored him.

Chester was the son of family friends, so I saw him occasionally over the years. Every moment is sealed in my mind in perfect clarity, every detail brilliant, every moment catalogued. It wasn't until many years later that Chester noticed me. I was nineteen and in college; Chester was twenty-four, working full-time, and living on his own. We were reintroduced at a reception following the memorial for his grandfather's death and quickly discovered we had a lot to talk about. The subjects ranged from photography to travel, and after that I don't remember much of what we discussed, but I know the conversation continued.

I was recovering from an unhealthy relationship. I had hesitated to call Chester for that very reason—I didn't want him to be a "rebound." But I felt compelled to call him, and after a few minutes of conversation I was laughing so hard my stomach ached. I realized that I hadn't laughed in a very long time. This was no rebound relationship; this was me finding life again. I quickly decided that I didn't want to stop having conversations with this handsome, intelligent, hilarious man.

We started dating and were married a year and a half later. Chester and I had a practical view of marriage. Neither of us imagined marriage was easy, and we were willing to work and sacrifice for the other. Because of that foundation, our first year of marriage was wonderful.

We fought often in our early years, but we always talked through things and grew and learned. What surprised me was that Chester was nearly always right. His logic was flawless, and he seemed to be able to pinpoint my errors with astonishing clarity. Being quick to find my own fault, I assumed I had married a man of impeccable character and an intellect that clearly surpassed my own. I began working at communicating and not overstepping his boundaries.

When we were dating we developed a love of long car rides. Conversation was easy, and the ebb and flow of subjects would keep us engaged for hours. We often had spirited debates. Once we had children, long road trips took on a different character. Frequent potty breaks, loud wailing from the back, and incessant demands for snacks made conversation more difficult. We preferred traveling at night. Once the kids were worn out from their antics and fell asleep, we rediscovered our love of discussion.

It was on one such road trip, driving home from a short vacation to the mountains, that Chester confessed to me he struggled with masturbation. While our four children dreamed in the back of the van, he explained what he felt most guilty about was that he sometimes fantasized about being with other women.

I remember looking at my bare feet on the dashboard as what he was saying sank in. I thought of the beautiful women we knew and wondered if he had fantasized about each one. I remembered how safe and confident I felt around other attractive women, because Chester had always seemed uninterested in how other women looked. He was scornful of men who pointed out how attractive women were. I had convinced myself that he was not as sexually and visually driven as other men. In a way, it gave me confidence. Even though my husband desired me less often than I would have liked, I assumed his desire was limited but fulfilled by only me.

I had created a false reality. I had been ignorant, and now

my so-called reality was fragmenting and falling apart. I was confused, and deep insecurities I thought had been laid to rest in my teen years reared their merciless heads. They began to pick away at my confidence in myself and in my marriage. I cried a lot on that drive, silently so as not to wake the children. All the while Chester was explaining that he knew his fantasies were rooted in a deep fear of intimacy. He said he had repented before God and couldn't lie to me anymore. When we got home, I told him I forgave him and, in tears, we made love.

Chester gave me permission to speak with a friend about what he had confessed. I knew Cameron's husband had struggled with an addiction to pornography, and I figured even though my situation was less intense, it would be safe to talk to her about what I was feeling.

As we talked and I explained Chester's confession, she casually asked, "And porn isn't a problem for him? In my experience men need something visual." I assured her that Chester had no issue with pornography—he struggled only with masturbation. She accepted my answer but regarded me with a look of mild disbelief.

I was surprised when her question stayed with me, buzzing around my mind like an annoying mosquito. I kept seeing the look in Cameron's eyes when I had assured her that porn was not a problem for Chester. Doubts crept in. Finally, I decided to ask Chester.

"Chester." We were in bed at this point—we lived with my parents, and our bedroom was the only place we could be alone. "I know you confessed having an issue with masturbation, but you never looked at porn, did you?"

There is something about silence when it follows such a question. That silence can scream at you that you have yet again been so wrong, so stupid in your assumptions. The seconds dragged on, and he uttered no emphatic denial. It was then I knew how wrong I had been. I was a fool.

"Yes," he answered finally. "I didn't think the pornography mattered. I thought I had confessed the worst of my betrayal and didn't want to add to it."

At this point there was a throbbing in my brain that became harder and harder to ignore. I was hit by so many emotions at once. I sat bolt upright in bed and then started to get up. "I'm so sorry, Elisa," Chester said tearfully. "I thought I wouldn't want to look at pornography anymore once we were married. I would make it for long periods without looking at it, and then I would go through periods where I used it all the time. Often I would look at porn to stop myself from fantasizing about someone other than you. I felt it was less of a betrayal."

Safe to say that any self-confidence that remained after the first confession was now shattered. I felt like every perfect moment I had ever experienced with Chester, every beautiful aspect of our love, was swept away. In the place of my tarnished memories were questions. Did he actually love me? Was I enough? Was he satisfied with me only because he had the option to escape into fantasy with perfect images? Could I ever trust him again? How could I have been such an idiot? How could I believe him when he said my post-baby body was wonderful and enough for him, when all the while he was having his pick of airbrushed perfection?

"Elisa, I am so sorry," my husband was saying tearfully, "I love you, I didn't want to hurt you. I didn't think the porn was important, but I see now that it was. I am sorry." With a strong act of the will I put a temporary hold on the questions that were tearing me into bits inside, because he needed a response.

I had the sense I was holding his heart in my hands. Here was my formerly emotionally distant husband humbly offering me something I had always wanted: himself. I had a choice. I could take his heart and crush it in my pain-fueled fury, or I could give him an undeserved gift. In those seconds I remember focusing on Christ, on what he had given me.

"I forgive you." The emotions were pulsing within me. "I forgive you, but I need to be alone."

Maybe if we had been in our own home I would have yelled at him, cursed, made him feel small. Perhaps I would have attempted to inflict a fraction of the pain I was feeling. Instead, due to our living situation, I was forced into solitude with God. I walked out of the house into a crisp fall evening. There were a million glorious stars twinkling above me, subtly reminding me of truths I would need.

I am thankful now that it was God who took my anger in that moment instead of my broken, insecure husband. In reality, it was God with whom I was most angry in all of this. And only he is big enough to handle the anguish and agonizing brokenness that this life holds. As much as he may hate to see us hurting, he hadn't prevented it, and it was for this reason he held the focus of my fury. This was the gist of my tirade—er, prayer.

"Are you f★★★★★★ kidding me, God?! Porn? Masturbation? Dreaming of women other than me? When I have always desired sex? I thought this man was what you wanted for me. I have strived to obey you. I have not been perfect, but I have loved you and desired to be in your will. And now I am here? How could you let this go on for eight years of marriage, when at any point I would have forgiven him? How could you let me wonder for so long what was wrong with me because I seemed to desire intimacy more often than my husband, and wonder why he seemed disinterested in me? It wasn't because he lacked desire—it was because he had satisfied himself, because he preferred that over me.

"I can't do this! I have given him everything, and it is not enough. I have loved him deeply and served him out of that love. I have shared my own struggles, been vulnerable, trusted him—and *you* implicitly—and I have been led like a lamb to the slaughter. How can I go on? There is nothing left of me. I am broken beyond repair. I can't do this! I can't do this! I need you, Jesus."

I sobbed for what seemed like hours but was most likely minutes. When I picked myself up, I knew that if I waited any longer to go back to my husband, I would never go. I wanted to run away from my life and never look back. With a final prayer for strength, I returned to my bed and my broken husband and forgave him.

The weeks that followed were a battle. I believe the second confession was the truth. When things are still hidden we cannot be fully in the light. After confessing to his addiction (though he didn't call it that) and receiving my forgiveness, Chester was a different person. He looked at me in a way I hadn't experienced since we were dating. I was the only person in the world to him. He beamed at me with such a light that I felt I could endure any pain, survive any agony. I began to sort through the emotions slowly, which is my way. Chester walked with me day by day, encouraging me and reassuring me. He constantly reminded me I was all he wanted. I began to rebuild my confidence and trust in him on the foundation of those words.

Chester encouraged me to ask him regularly how he was doing with his struggle with lust, masturbation, and porn. He put an accountability program on his computer and phone. I did not ask anything of him after the first confession. I allowed him to decide what he needed to do to protect himself. I did ask after several weeks of being his accountability partner if he would also have a man in his life as a second accountability partner. I was concerned about the pressure it put me under to be the only person checking in on him. He complied without question.

We made many practical changes in our life. We stopped watching movies unless we had checked the rating on a parent-friendly website. We stopped watching television except the occasional unobjectionable show. Chester read to me in the evenings, and we spent a lot of time talking, which usually led to physical intimacy. I began to lose weight. The stress took its physical form in a lack of desire to eat, which was nice because being thinner and healthier helped rebuild my self-confidence.

I began to believe that Chester's problem could be solved by his being known fully and accepted by me and by my complete willingness to meet his physical needs. It helped that sex made me feel safe and fully loved. It also seemed to provide healing to both of us.

My relationship with God didn't grow much during this time. I talked to him and I wrote many prayers in my journal. I realized that I was much angrier at God than I first realized. It took me a long time to figure out that I blamed him more than Chester for how long this sin stayed hidden in our marriage. I knew God could have allowed Chester to be found out at any point.

It took a while, but I came to understand that God had allowed the lies to stay hidden until Chester couldn't live with it and was compelled to tell me. I have since learned that this is a blessing—many women do not get the gift of a confession but instead are forced to find the evidence and confront a potentially unrepentant man.

Six months passed, and Chester had not expressed a desire to look at porn. We moved from my parents' house to a new state and city. We had our own house and began to find our own rhythms as a family. It was a stressful yet joyful time. We found a church community and began to make friends. I felt more and more confident in our relationship. We had moved past the initial period of Chester constantly affirming me, but we stayed connected and made love regularly. I assumed the problem was solved.

After being in our new home for several months, I decided to visit a family member overnight. Chester agreed to stay home with our four children so I could get some much needed time alone. It was such a refreshing trip. On my early-morning drive home, I stopped at a coffee shop. Chester called me just as I sat down to enjoy my cappuccino. I answered my phone cheerfully but was stunned into silence. He was sobbing,

"Elisa, last night I looked at porn and masturbated." It took me a moment to figure out what he said. "I'm so sorry. I wanted to tell you before you got home. I know you have several hours of driving left, and I thought it better to let you process instead of telling you when you get back to the kids."

"I forgive you. I love you. I will see you in a couple of hours." I was so calm in the moment, but I could feel the panic and despair setting in. He told me he loved me and that he was sorry again before he got off the phone. I sat and drank my cappuccino in silence, staring off into space.

I was thankful he chose to tell me on the phone so I had the drive back to process the information. I pinballed between sobbing and complete numbness. My thoughts, though not wholly unhealthy, rambled along, sinking into deeper and deeper ruts of hopelessness. I started to think, "If that is what he really wants, let him have it!" I called my friend Cameron, and she prayed with me. By the time I got home, I had collected myself enough to get through the week. We had planned to get away for the weekend without the kids, and I knew I would have more time to process then.

Our getaway was hard, but perfectly timed. It felt like a gift from God placed at exactly the right moment. I had a frightening realization: Chester still desired pornography. This struggle within him went deep and would not be going away any time soon. No amount of sex, lost weight on my part, or meeting his needs would change him.

I was out of control. My confidence again was shattered; I had built it on a foundation of sand. The only thing I could hold onto was that he had told me; he had been honest and repentant and had confessed immediately. It was small comfort, but at least I could trust him in that.

At one point during the weekend, I had to get space, so I went for a walk. I didn't even put on shoes. I ran across a small road and crossed a bridge over a beautiful tributary to reach the beach, where I ran out onto the sand. It was a chilly spring evening. The sun had set. I walked beside the breaking waves and cried out to God in my pain.

Jealous anger overwhelmed me. I was not a woman denying her husband intimacy. I delighted in connecting with him, and I wanted every part of our marriage to be pure. Every time he chose to indulge himself sexually, he was denying me what was mine. Our bodies were part of our covenant.

In a split second, I was hit with a message so pure and bright it stopped me in my tracks. It was as if God spoke directly to my heart as I stood barefoot in the wind with the waves gently washing over my feet.

"Oh, Elisa, don't you understand? This anger you feel is just and right. It is what I feel every time you take what is mine and squander it. I feel this jealousy every time a life I created is lived for the glory of something or someone other than me. You are getting a glimpse into my heart for you."

I started crying again, this time out of guilt, feeling I was given a tiny picture of what my God feels when I worship idols instead of him. He gave humanity himself, and we bumble along, unable to see beyond ourselves. I confessed all the things I had placed before him and praised him for his faithfulness. This is an excerpt from the journal I wrote after my walk.

> A light breaks through the greasy black
> The unquenchable flame
> Born to perfect death
> Here to conquer; victory over sin
> This light calls me home
> My Jesus, perfect sacrifice
> Strip me of myself that I may know you more
> That I may reflect your light
> unto the world.

We returned home feeling disheartened. Yes, we had connected and made some progress in understanding the nature of Chester's struggle and the depth of the wounds, but we had a long road ahead. We went back to real life unprepared for how hard it would be. I cried out to God daily, begging for healing. I didn't feel like this experience had made me stronger—on the contrary, it made me into a broken, insecure, irrationally emotional, semi-crazy person.

As the weeks passed, Chester and I hashed out many things from before his first confession. I realized that when I forgave him, I had no idea what I was forgiving. It was similar to the way when you vow to love someone through the good and the bad you have no clue what you are vowing. I might be dealing with confessions every six months for the rest of my marriage.

I took my wedding ring off for a few days as I forced myself to face this reality. Was I at peace with the vow I had made? I felt like if I decided I was, it would be like walking into the line of fire, knowing more bullets would rip through my body. I didn't know if I would be able to take the pain. After several days of praying, I put my ring back on. If God had been there for me so far, I could trust him to continue to be there for me.

One day Chester informed me, very matter-of-factly, that he had realized he had no obligation to tell me anything about his struggle, even if he chose to indulge in porn and mastur-bation again. It was his struggle, and I had nothing to do with it. Thus, in one conversation I was stripped of my last shred of safety in our relationship.

The following months were a rollercoaster. I was plagued by fears that he had returned to his old way of living. He refused to let me in on how he was doing. The thought of being blindsided or being lied to again was terrifying. I tried to hide the emotions I was feeling out of fear he would pull away further. Nothing helped.

I found a ray of light in reading the Bible and praying. I praised God for who he was when I didn't have the space to praise him for what I was experiencing. I felt like I was hang-ing on by a thread. I felt I couldn't live without Chester and I was going to lose him—either he was going to choose porn or someone else over me, or my emotional chaos was going to drive him away.

To add to my insecurities, Chester was going overseas on a business trip. I was going to be home alone with the four children for fourteen days, and my husband was going to be in another time zone on the other side of the world. I knew this trip would hit Chester with every one of his triggers: physical exertion, stress, and a potential feeling of failure—not to mention being alone in a hotel room for two weeks. I knew he would be struggling every night, and when I asked if he would keep me updated on how he was doing, he said no. It was a terrifying thought.

I didn't push him. I felt like God was telling me I needed to let Chester go on this trip and succeed or fail on his own in his battle against sin. I prayed fervently before he left, and we had several hard conversations about his struggles and about my own issues with communication and trust. In the end, no amount of conversation could have prepared me for Chester being gone that long.

Four days in, after horrible communication with Chester and many intense episodes with unruly children, I broke down and surrendered. I had nothing left. I didn't have even the illusion of control over any aspect of my life. I admitted my lack of control and confessed to God that it terrified me. When I had no more words to pray, I borrowed those of David from the Psalms.

"Save me, O God! For the waters have come up to my neck. I sink in deep mire, where there is no foothold; I have come into deep waters, and the flood sweeps over me. I am weary with my crying out; my throat is parched. My eyes grow dim with waiting for my God" (Ps. 69:1).

It was in this dark moment that I released Chester completely and threw myself on Christ's mercy. That was the turning point in my journey, though there was no amazing change from that moment in my marriage. No, the change was in me: I finally realized that I had made Chester an idol. I relied on him to make me feel secure, loved, and protected. Any human would fail in this. Only one could sustain me, one who had paid the ultimate sacrifice to purchase me from death. I found a new life and a new perspective.

During the rest of the time Chester was gone, I spent most of my down time alone. I read my Bible, prayed, and read a book titled *Undefiled: Redemption from Sexual Sin, Restoration for Broken Relationships* that provided much wisdom and enlightenment. It validated the pain I had experienced and illuminated the fact that nothing I could do would change my husband. He needed Christ to change him.

When I share my story with people (or ask their reaction to pornography), they respond typically in one of two ways. Some downplay the gravity of pornography/masturbation by calling it a "man thing," just a leftover of our animalistic, evolutionary roots that should be tolerated or ignored. Others seem to want to "lock it down," to deal with the issue by controlling the action: "Your husband needs to find sobriety."

The first response is frustrating, to say the least. It leaves no room for my dignity and my right—let alone God's right—to my husband's heart and body. As much as I understand the second view, there's still something missing. I could threaten, demand more control over our Internet and my husband's computer, check his browsing history, force him to go to meetings, threaten to withhold sex—the list goes on. Yet the deep root of all sexual sin is in the heart. I knew that my husband's choices were a reflection of something much deeper and that preventing the action would not mean my husband was healed. I think this quote clearly illustrates the point:

> "The drive to 'look' isn't an overpowering sex drive or an addiction to sex, but an overpowering, demanding, selfish desire. Pornography, with its inherent ability to be secretive with easy accessibility, uniquely meets that demand. The essence of your husband's condition is an unwillingness to be told what to do spiritually, relationally, and sexually. You need a new man, not just a change in behavior."[2]

2. Excerpt from an article by Dr. Harry Schaumberg: restoringsexualpurity.org/your-husband-looks-at-porn-now-what/

When Chester got back from his business trip, it turned out he had looked at porn several times. I cried and was angry, but the emotions passed much more quickly than before. It helped that I was no longer building my confidence on my husband's perfection but on Christ. I spent a lot of time in prayer, and slowly Chester started opening up to me again.

It was clear that, as much as he fought it, my husband still wanted pornography. I knew that I had no control over my husband's desire and choices. What my husband needed was not threats or boundaries but a heart change. I chose yet again to not demand anything of Chester.

Don't get me wrong. When you are dealing with addiction, it is crucial to protect yourself by removing temptations. But my husband had to make those decisions on his own. If I were to tell him to delete an application from his phone, he would feel trapped, and it would not lead to a heart change. Instead, I did what was probably the most difficult task of my journey: turn control—or at least my illusion of and attempt to control—over to Christ. I began to live by this verse:

> "Likewise, wives, be subject to your own husbands, so that even if some do not obey the word, they may be won without a word by the conduct of their wives, when they see your respectful and pure conduct. Do not let your adorning be external—the braiding of hair and the putting on of gold jewelry, or the clothing you wear—but let your adorning be the hidden person of the heart with the imperishable beauty of a gentle and quiet spirit, which in God's sight is very precious" (1 Pet. 3:1-4).

The other beautiful thing that came out of this choice to release my husband to Christ was that I fell in love with Chester in a new way. I saw that he was lost, choosing his own will over God's, as I often did myself. I was able to focus on the wonderful things about him: he is hard-working and loves me deeply; he is a devoted father and always my best friend. I had lost sight of how incredible he was because his struggles had been my focus.

I started learning more about prayer, and I had a new way to intercede. I began daily to take my fear, anger, and woundedness to the cross in prayer. I started praying for my husband to have a changed heart. I stopped asking how he was doing with his struggles and instead I asked how he was feeling and what he was thinking. I listened with a God-given detachment to his fears about work, our marriage, and the kids. I was able to care for his wounds, because I had given mine to Christ.

Instead of asking him to delete apps off his phone that I knew were a problem, I asked him to pray with me every night before we went to bed and read a short devotional every morning with me. We started a once-a-week study of the book *Undefiled*. The study gave us a space to talk through some hard questions and begin to process healthily our individual and collective need for redemption.

Through this study my eyes were opened to the ways I had allowed sin to exist in my life, either because the sins were small or seemed justified. I began to confess to Christ my fears, self-pity, and my desire to control my life. I began to ask questions of myself: Was I being like Christ? Was I living in my woundedness and self-pity instead of living in the forgiveness I had found in Christ? Was I living in my commitment to my marriage and loving my husband, not for my own comfort but for God's glory?

Redemption is often an agonizingly slow process. In spite of that, it is amazing now to look at how much Chester and I have changed. We recently passed the date that marks a year since his first confession. We are not perfect, and we still have very hard conversations. I am under no illusion that my husband is "healed" and he will not ever choose porn and masturbation over real intimacy with me. I choose not to think about my husband's potential to fail. Instead, I acknowledge his human weakness before the Lord, and I do battle daily for him in prayer—not for my own sake but for his sake and out of obedience to and love of Christ.

I still get bogged down by my fears and insecurities. I feel valueless and pointless at times. If Chester is working on a project and we aren't able to connect regularly, I often fall into an emotional tailspin. I assume something is horribly wrong with our relationship and we are headed for failure. The difference is, I recognize it for what it is: not trusting Christ. I have begun to notice much more quickly what it looks like when I start down that emotional path, and I am faster at casting my burdens on Christ, who is able to handle them.

There have been many victories for me in this journey. One of the most important has been the ability to thank God for my trials. I have started to see how God gently used them to move me closer to him and to refine me. I have a relationship—no, a life—with Chester I wouldn't have had if I had not been brought to a place of complete reliance on God and his mercy. Chester has a relationship with God that has progressed without me trying to help it along or control it.

My husband and I have an incredible relationship that has been forged in the crucible of sexual sin. We love being together and spend most evenings reading, talking, and playing games. On date nights, we enjoy a beer and fries at the local pub and stare at each other and smile. We talk about our fears and our hopes and dreams. We hold hands and kiss every day and make love often. Honestly, I don't think I could imagine to ask for more than this. I am thankful and blessed that God gave me a husband who is so much better than the man of my dreams.

"Many waters cannot quench love, neither can floods drown it. If a man offered for love all the wealth of his house, it would be utterly scorned" (Song of Sol. 8:7).

Afflicted but Not Broken

It used to be thought that porn was merely a "guy thing," something women didn't struggle with. This is a myth, but it's one that is still widely believed and taught in Christian circles. Who does a wife turn to, then, when she's a willing participant in the thing that is destroying her marriage? Many counselors would tell her that so long as it's consensual it's fine, and even healthy, while many people in the Church—I'm sad to say— would react with awkwardness at best, disgust and judgment at worst. Pornography, by its very nature, is unable to satisfy our deep yearning for love and intimacy. It may excite us, it may give us a thrill, but it doesn't deliver on the joy we were certain it was promising. Because of this, the porn addict always has to up the ante. And when a couple is watching porn, this can lead their sex life, which God desires to be holy and beautiful, into some dark places. Here Christina beautifully and articulately shares how porn did just that, and how, by the grace of God and solid friendships, she and her husband were able to climb back out of the filth they had plunged into and restore their relationship with God and each other.

—MATT

My world fell apart February 15, 2013. I had been arguing with my husband all day. He was edgy and distant and obsessed with trying to fix our old Dodge so he could go out of town to visit friends. We sat in the living room, me in an armchair, he at the desk. After a period of silence, I finally asked him what was really bothering him, not believing that car troubles were why he had been so distant.

He sat still for a moment then quietly said he didn't think he loved me anymore. I stared at him, uncomprehending, and asked him to repeat what he had said. He did. Inexplicably, the color red flashed through my mind, and anger took over. I jumped up, ran into the bedroom, threw all his clothes into the hallway, and yelled at him to get out of my house.

He had walked into the kitchen to wash his hands, which were still covered with grease from working on the car. I marched into the kitchen and snatched the kitchen towel out of his hand. I demanded to know why. Why, after eleven years of marriage, did he suddenly believe he didn't love me anymore?

He stood staring at me, not saying a word. The anger boiled over, and I shoved him. He fell backward. I was shocked at what I had done. Never had either of us physically harmed the other.

My husband was as shocked as I was. After a moment, he said in a shaky voice, "I've been lying to you. I've been lying for six years." It dawned on me that the truth was finally going to come out. I was finally going to understand why the past six years of our marriage had been so difficult and why we seemed like strangers to each other instead of loving partners. I held onto the kitchen counter and steadied myself for the blow. He said, "I've been having an affair."

I see my marriage as consisting of two time periods: before disclosure and after disclosure. The day my husband told me about his secret life, it was almost like a line was drawn in time. The marriage I had been in, the marriage that had lasted for eleven years, was over. The marriage I was currently in, the one that began February 15, was just beginning. Slowly, over the course of five weeks, my husband also admitted to being addicted to pornography and masturbation. This was a foreign concept to me. How could anyone be addicted to something you watch on TV or online? How could anyone be addicted to pleasing themselves?

I grew up in a multigenerational, multicultural home. My father and mother had married because my mother was pregnant with my brother. My father didn't want to marry my mother because he was having too much fun with his many girlfriends; but under pressure from his family he finally agreed.

We lived in a home with my father's family, including my grandfather, grandmother, and uncle. As a child, I was sexually abused by this uncle. The abuse, which robbed me of my childhood and destroyed any sense of safety I felt, lasted from when I was about five years old until I was about eleven. My parents were emotionally unavailable to me. My father busied himself with his many addictions (alcohol, food, and sex), and my mother, the codependent wife, busied herself with obsessing about my father.

I was exposed to pornography at a very young age. My father had magazines in the garage and kept video tapes in his dresser drawer. My older brother, who I believe was also sexually abused, would play the videos for his friends while my younger sister and I quietly watched from the corner of the living room. I learned that pornography was normal, that it was part of adult life, and that sometimes it was fun to watch.

I met my husband online, right after I ended a six-year relationship with an abusive man whom I worshipped. My husband was flirty, smart, and shy. I was immediately attracted to him, and after three months of intense e-mailing and a few short phone calls, we decided to meet in person. Within forty-five minutes of meeting, we were in bed. Two months later, we were living together.

One night, after finding pornography on our home computer, I encouraged my future husband to watch it with me, hoping that he would be excited by my openness. I knew I could never compete with the thin, beautiful women in those pornographic films. The only thing I could offer was use of my body while he watched sexual fantasy being played out on TV.

That began a regular habit for us. It almost seemed as if we couldn't make love without "warming up" with pornography or watching it during the act. Still, it never bothered me; I saw pornography as part of a normal relationship. Four months after moving in together, we got married.

Pornography became a part of our marriage. We visited adult video stores together, sometimes two or three times a week. We shopped at stores that sold adult products, and we spent quite a bit of money on products we saw being used in the pornographic films we were watching. As time passed, my husband seemed to get bored with what we were doing, and so I'd suggest new things in the hopes of retaining his sexual interest.

I was terrified that if I wasn't sexually adventurous, he'd leave me, as boyfriends had done in the past. I learned from my family of origin that a woman's job was to sexually please her man, and if she didn't, he had a right to look for sexual gratification elsewhere.

Soon pornographic films, websites, and magazines were no longer enough. I knew my husband's ultimate fantasy was to add another woman to our marriage. After struggling with jealous feelings and the emotional pain of thinking of my husband with another woman, I agreed.

We started a relationship with a woman that lasted for about six months. It ended disastrously when I could no longer swallow the jealousy. My husband and I committed to ending all contact with her, and I thought we could simply put this experiment behind us and move on with our marriage. But something was changing inside of me. I knew I could no longer keep up the pace of our sexual exploits. Something had to give.

I was raised in the Catholic Faith as a child, but as a teenager I left the Church. As an adult, I believed in some kind of God but wanted nothing to do with organized religion. After the relationship with our extra partner ended, I started to yearn for God. The life I was leading was empty and brought me no spiritual joy. I wanted to take another look at the Catholic Church and see if I could fit in.

Once I decided I wanted to go back to the Faith of my childhood, I spoke to my husband and ended all viewing of pornography. I wanted to live a chaste life, and I knew pornography was hurting me. My husband, who was cynical about religion, agreed to stop looking at pornography and humored my reentrance into the Catholic Faith.

My husband had been distant with me for a while. He would come home from work, yell at me about something or another, and then drink himself to sleep with a six-pack of beer. I wanted desperately for my marriage to work, and so I took his criticisms to heart. I changed my clothes, my hair, my job, how I decorated the house, even my hobbies. Nothing seemed to please him.

When he decided to stop drinking, I thought it would be a turning point. I hoped my husband would recover from his alcoholism and return to his former, loving self.

But it never happened. I kept making excuses for his behavior, telling myself that anyone recovering from a drinking problem would act the way he did. Our lovemaking became rare. The only time we made love was if I attracted his attention by hinting at the old pornographic fantasies. I felt disgusted with myself but rationalized my behavior—I wasn't sinning because I was staying within the bounds of my marriage. My husband and I continued to argue and spend more time apart, and, in the end, we became like roommates who simply tolerated each other.

The first few days after my husband told me about his affair, I was numb. I didn't know if I was going to stay married; I didn't know if my husband really meant it when he said he had ended the affair; and I didn't know if trust and love could ever be restored.

I was surfing the Internet for resources on infidelity when I came across an article about addiction to pornography. The article had a few websites listed at the end, and I clicked on one of the links. It was for a twelve-step program that specialized in helping people with sex addiction, including addiction to pornography. I read the twenty or so questions listed to help people identify as a sex addict and I found my husband in almost every one. I told my husband about the program, and we agreed that he should attend a meeting.

What a blessing this twelve-step program has been in our lives. My husband left his first meeting absolutely stunned. He said he had just met twenty-five different versions of himself, and he had to admit out loud that he was a sex addict. He found a sponsor, started working the twelve steps, and, by the divine power of God, decided to convert to Catholicism. He was getting better. His old self was coming back; he was more loving, more patient, and he never failed to hold me when I cried and grieved over his betrayal. God was working a miracle in my husband's life, but something wasn't right. My husband was healing, but I wasn't.

I became obsessed with monitoring my husband. I checked his e-mail several times a day. I demanded he hand over his cell phone when he came home from work so that I could check his text messages. I systematically searched out and destroyed every shred of pornography on our computer, on my husband's laptop, on his cell phone, and in our home. I did daily checks of the computer to make sure no pornography had been downloaded.

I found horrifying things, proof that my husband's sex addiction had progressed. His porn viewing had run the gamut from gender-bending to sexual violence and back again. Every new discovery would send me into a fit of rage, and I would throw plates, cups, and anything breakable in my empty garage. Hearing the sound of breaking glass on the cement calmed my rage and allowed me to process the feelings of repulsion and anger.

I started having flashbacks to the moment of disclosure and I would melt down into a ball of crying fury. My husband had made the mistake of disclosing details of his affair to me, and I spent hours obsessing over them, playing in my head a pornographic version of what had happened.

I tortured myself for months, sought counseling, and isolated myself from my family, friends, and coworkers. I stopped praying and turned my anger toward God. How could he do this to me? I had just found my way back to the Catholic Church when God threw me this curveball. It was too much for me. I was living in hell, and I was convinced God didn't care enough to rescue me.

My husband told me he wanted to start attending a meeting for his program that was held on Sunday nights. He said there was a meeting at the same time for a companion program for people who were affected by someone else's sex addiction. Was I interested in attending? He said we could drive together, go to our respective meetings, and see if they were helpful. I was doubtful but I went anyway, more out of a desire to keep an eye on him than to seek help myself.

We arrived early and I found a woman sitting on the floor outside the meeting room waiting for someone to unlock the door. She asked if this was my first time at the meeting. I said it was and started quizzing her about the program. She said members were encouraged to work the twelve steps.

I demanded to know why I had to work the steps if my husband was the one with the problem. She smiled and explained that people who are affected by another person's sex addiction have their own progressive spiritual illness. She said that working the steps would help me reconnect with my higher power and help me find serenity. I rolled my eyes, but by that time the door was open and the meeting was starting.

I don't remember much about that first meeting. I remember I spoke—I may have even cried—but I don't remember what I said or what I heard. But I kept coming back. Week after week I'd show up, dump my ugly feelings onto the group, and leave feeling lighter. I was surprised by how angry my "shares" were. I didn't realize how much rage was inside of me until I started to let some of it go.

One night, after a meeting where I cried, one of the women asked if I had a sponsor. I said no, and she asked if she could help me start working the twelve steps. I jumped at the chance. For weeks I had been hearing women sing the praises of the twelve steps, and when they shared about how close they felt to their higher power, I was envious. I wanted what they had but didn't know how to get it. My sponsor was willing to show me.

When I look back at how much I leaned on her, I feel

deep gratitude for her patience. This woman took me under her wing, taught me concepts like "boundaries" and "self-care," listened as I wailed on the phone, hurting from the deep pain I was processing, and took time out of her busy life as a married mother of two young boys to walk me through the program of recovery. Our early conversations would go something like this:

> *Me:* I'm calling to let you know that my husband did not show me the same amount of affection tonight when he got home from work as he did last night, and I'm convinced that he's watching pornography and having another affair. I'm leaving him.
> *Sponsor:* Wow, do you want to talk about it?
> *Me:* What's there to talk about? I'm leaving him.
> *Sponsor:* Maybe we should talk about this.
> *Me:* Fine. You talk.

My sponsor would talk to me until I calmed down and saw how irrationally I was acting. She encouraged me to keep the focus on myself and not worry about what my husband was doing. How was *I* doing? What was *I* feeling? I could not control my husband's actions or words; all I could control was my reaction to him. She taught me how to respond, not react, and how to take time out for myself when I was feeling "triggered." She taught me about triggers!

With the help of the counselor I was seeing, I started working on healing from my childhood sexual abuse. I learned to confront the lessons I had been taught in childhood: my body was not my own, I was valuable only when a man was lusting after me, pornography was an essential part of any sexual relationship.

I got in touch with my inner child and made friends with

her. I spent time coloring, reading children's books, watching cartoons, and playing games. One afternoon I got the idea that my inner child needed a teddy bear, so I bought one at a thrift store. When I got home I noticed that the bear I had chosen was from a local children's hospital and was given to sick children who might have been feeling scared. I knew that God had given me this teddy bear. He wanted me to let him back into my life.

Months after I had cast my rosary aside in anger, I picked it up again and prayed. I found a book in my local library that was about being angry with God. The author reassured me that God could handle my anger and that working through my anger would end in a deeper relationship with him. I started journaling and talking in my meetings about my anger at God. My sponsor told me to keep praying, to keep asking God to help me forgive him.

Little by little, I started letting God back into my life. I started giving him my smaller worries, and when I saw that he had helped me with those, I gave him larger worries. God, just like my husband, was working to show he loved me and wanted me to trust him again.

I have learned that the road to recovery isn't an unbroken path of progress. There's a reason the twelve-step program's slogan is "Progress, not perfection." After months of progress, I started sliding into depression. The anniversary of my husband's disclosure was approaching and I was dreading the emotional toll I knew it was going to take on me. I was having more flashbacks, isolating myself more, and doing poorly at work. I even contemplated suicide, going as far as visualizing myself driving off a bridge or driving into an oncoming semi-truck. I wanted the pain to end, and it seemed that nothing else could give me relief.

On a whim, I decided to go to Mass at a church I rarely attended. The music was beautiful, the church was warm and cozy, and the people seemed happy to be there. The new priest had already made a name for himself with his plans to evangelize the city and bring people to the Church. As I sat in the pew, I listened to his message and found myself listening to God's voice.

The priest pondered the kinds of troubles the people in the pews might have had on their hearts that night. He mentioned divorce, unruly teens, money problems, infidelity, and addiction. He talked about the independent spirit some people had and how they thought it was useless asking God for help. In a comforting voice, he said, "I'm here to tell you something. You don't have to be afraid. Everything is going to be okay."

I returned home that night reassured that God was walking this difficult path with me. My mood improved, and I was able to face the anniversary of my husband's disclosure calmly. My husband, on the other hand, a few days after his one-year anniversary of sexual sobriety, could not resist looking at pornographic images of his affair partner that he found buried deep in one of his e-mail folders.

This was my opportunity to practice keeping my boundaries, taking care of my own emotional needs, and turning my worries over to God. My husband renewed his efforts to work his program, changed his sponsor, and buckled down to work his steps. I was scared, but I kept praying, and I kept working my program of recovery. I made it through that trial shaken but not broken.

What is it like living with a sex addict? Life is certainly not the way it used to be. Because our society is so preoccupied with sex, we find that we're unable to do many of the things we used to do before recovery. Going to see a movie can be a bit dicey, unless it's G-rated. So many movies made for adults have sex scenes, pornographic images, sexual talk, or immodest dress. Any of these elements can trigger someone addicted to pornography. We avoid shopping malls and swimming pools, and our date nights consist of going for walks in the park instead of seeing the latest indie band. We canceled cable and ended up selling our TV. We don't buy magazines.

Before you think my husband and I spend our evenings staring at the walls, let me tell you how we spent the past few weekends. We attended a tour of ten homes that have model trains running in their gardens; we worked on our own garden, constructing raised beds and repairing the backyard fence; we attended a barbecue at a friend's house; we shopped the local yard sales; we wrote a poem for the neighborhood kids in chalk on our front sidewalk; and we lay in bed and read Harry Potter to each other.

My husband and I cook together, share a hobby room together, and pray together. We have long, deep, intimate talks. That was never possible when pornography was in our life. Life was always about getting the next sexual high, trying to please an insatiable partner, and trying to control and manipulate. Now our life is about enjoying being around each other and working hard to keep the evils of sex addiction out of our marriage.

We have had to make major changes in our sex life. In our pre-disclosure marriage, my husband watched Internet pornography on a daily basis and gratified himself sexually while filled with images of lust. He brought those images of lust (along with memories of his affair) into our marriage bed. It took him a while to confess that, even after disclosure, he was still doing this. I had to make the hard decision not to have sex with my husband while he continued to have these kinds of fantasies. Lust does not belong in a marriage.

With the help of a marriage counselor, we examined what

sex meant to each of us. My husband saw it as a sign of approval, and his self-esteem hinged on it; I saw it as love and based my self-worth on it. We had to learn what it meant to be intimate, and this meant finding ways that did not involve sex. I had to learn to say no to sex, to quiet my fears, and to honor my boundaries by taking care of myself and reaching out to my program fellows for help.

I have learned much from my recovery of being affected by sex addiction. I have been able to forgive my husband. I also confronted my uncle who had sexually abused me, and he apologized. It was then up to me to forgive. With God's help, I was able to do so.

I have forgiven my parents for being emotionally unavailable and for instilling in me such dysfunctional messages about sex and relationships. I have forgiven my past boyfriends and the various people throughout my life who have hurt me. Most importantly, I have forgiven myself. Forgiveness isn't about the other person; it's about releasing the hurt inside and allowing God to fill the space it leaves. Through the sacrament of confession I received God's forgiveness for my sins.

Addiction is a progressive disease. What was a fun way to spice up our sex life turned into a nightmare. My husband's need for sexual stimulation grew until pornographic pictures could no longer satisfy his lust. He sought out real-life pornography in the form of our extra partner and his affair. I have known other sex addicts who started out with pornography and, as their disease progressed, began having affairs, picking up prostitutes, and even experimenting with homosexuality. Without help, this disease only gets worse.

My husband's addiction started with watching images on a TV screen or seeing images in a magazine that could be recalled in an instant to satisfy his craving for another "lust hit." These images are not harmless like our society claims they are.

Pornography alters the mind physically, distorts what sex and love really are, and traps the viewer into wanting more and more. Lust only grows stronger, and the one thing that can stop it is a recovery program anchored in reliance on God.

I speak out when I can about the evils of pornography and our sex-obsessed culture. Recently, I posted an article on a social media website about women in pornographic films and how they suffer from exploitation, sex trafficking, drug abuse, and even sexual torture. A family member replied that women in pornographic films seem happy and that these films, at worst, are simply a necessary evil, especially for married couples. I felt sad for this person, but it was a good reminder of why I need to continue to speak out.

Lust has such a grip on our culture that it seems normal to indulge in such unhealthy behavior. I can't even walk around a shopping mall without being bombarded with images of half-naked models staring at me from the shop windows. When friends want to meet at the mall for lunch, I either suggest an alternative or I simply turn them down. I am not shy about my distaste of pornographic images, and I refuse to expose myself to things that could harm my serenity.

An unexpected benefit of working a program of recovery is the fellowship. I remember how angry I felt during my first few meetings. I had no interest in befriending any of the "crazy" women who shared their stories every week. Only after surrendering did I come to enjoy and appreciate my fellows and the support they gave me.

I had never been able to be completely who I am—not at work, not in my family of origin, not even with my husband, especially when he was in his illness. Now I can be myself with my fellows, and I am still loved. I can be angry and shouting or I can be crying and feeling sorry for myself, but my fellows will be there for me, no matter what. I am loved for my humor, my intelligence, my kind heart, and my willingness to be there for them.

Having fellows takes me out of my own head and my own problems and reminds me that I'm not the center of the universe. My fellows ground me, reminding me that there are people who are hurting just like I am and that together we can recover from the effects of sex addiction. I don't have to do this alone.

As I continue my daily walk down the path of recovery, I know that God is my constant companion in my journey of healing. I am stronger than I was; wiser, more forgiving and compassionate, and less fearful. Recovery is about me, not my husband. Yes, my husband needed to seek his own path of recovery, but he wasn't the only sick one in our marriage. I had to admit defeat, surrender to the awesome power of God, and experience his mercy in my life. I needed to be restored.

Throughout my journey of healing, I have made it a point to speak to newcomers. Their pain reminds me of the beginnings of my journey, and the love and compassion I feel for them allows me to share myself and give back what has been given to me. If my story can convey one message, I would want it to be this: You don't have to be afraid. Everything is going to be okay.

Forgive and Forgive Again

By MIMI AND MATT

Our Lord Jesus Christ commands us to forgive. He doesn't merely suggest it. He even goes so far as to say, "If you do not forgive men their trespasses, neither will your Father forgive your trespasses" (Matt. 6:15). Many of us wrongly assume that forgiveness means feeling a certain way, or we think forgiveness amounts to admitting, "It doesn't matter, it's not a big deal." Neither of these things is true. Forgiveness is not an emotional response (if it were, we couldn't praise it as a virtue, but an act of the will). And it isn't the same thing as saying, "It's okay." It's not okay! If it were, there would be nothing to forgive. The Catechism puts it beautifully: "It is not in our power not to feel or to forget an offense; but the heart that offers itself to the Holy Spirit turns injury into compassion and purifies the memory in transforming the hurt into intercession" (2843). Mimi and Matt share what it was like dealing with Matt's porn addiction and how Mimi, despite having been hurt by Matt's behavior, chose to forgive him anyway; and how, eventually, our Lord brought (and continues to bring) healing to those hurting places in Mimi's heart.

—MATT

Mimi: I had the advantage of knowing my husband's struggle with masturbation and pornography before we even dated. After two years of a college friendship, one night we opened up to each other and shared our histories and struggles. We started dating soon after that, and most of the time we dated, we didn't talk about his fight with porn again. So, while I was surprised when he told me years later that he still struggled to stop watching pornography, it didn't catch me totally off guard. Because of my own limitations with a different addiction—food—I was able to be compassionate and forgiving toward Matt.

For much of my life, my "drug" of choice was food. I have a very personal experience of wishing I could stop a behavior and finding it tremendously hard to do so. Leading up to our engagement, I could accept that he made it two weeks, fell, then three weeks, fell, then a month, fell, then a week, fell, etc. Matt said that I set the expectation for better but never judged him.

I found solace in Matt's efforts and progress, even during the times he took a step back. I had patience with how long it was taking to be fully rid of pornography, because I knew how long it took me to gain control of eating habits that were destroying my soul. I accepted him for where he was in his fight. But most importantly, having lived the experience of an addiction wielding power over the body, mind, and spirit, I understood that his struggle with pornography was not a reflection of him not loving me enough. It was not a reflection of me being unlovable.

Matt: In December of 2012, I proposed to Mimi. By this time, I was in the upswing of ridding masturbation from my life. Almost two years before, I had learned that watching enough pornography can lead to erectile dysfunction. Combined with finally accepting God as my first love and wanting to be the best version of myself for my future bride, I was motivated enough to drop pornography from my life for six months. But still, the addiction of masturbation lingered, and after those six months, the porn returned. Until we started our pre-Cana marriage prep meetings with our priest the following January, I figured the addiction would be a part of my life forever.

Mimi: I remember during our first pre-Cana meeting our priest started with one daunting question: "How are you with forgiveness?" Shocked by the bluntness of his question, I replied, "Pretty good." I then proceeded to give some background of my family history. "But, of course," I concluded, "I know it's kind of a continual choice to forgive. Because it still hurts sometimes, so I still have to choose to forgive. And that's just a cross I'll have to bear."

I thought I was being wise, and was surprised by his response. "No, it doesn't work like that. It shouldn't hurt forever."

"What?"

"Think of a scar you have from an injury," he said. "It's a mark left on you from that wound, but if you scratch it, it doesn't hurt anymore, right? And if you scratch it and it still hurts, we would say that the injury still hasn't healed."

"Okay . . ."

"So when you talk about your family member, and that it still hurts sometimes, that means the wound isn't fully healed. But it can be healed, and when it is, it won't hurt anymore. Do you see what I'm saying?"

"Um . . . no. Sorry. I don't think I get it. Are you saying that this struggle, this wound, that I've had for my entire life, and have basically dealt with except for maybe just a tiny bit, can go away?"

"Yes. And before you get married."

It was really hard to believe him. But, still, I was in marriage prep, and I knew I wanted to bring as little baggage into our marriage as possible. So I figured that even if I could get the hurt from two percent to one percent, it was worth the effort.

Matt: The priest focused on Mimi and encouraged her to confront the wounds of her past. He told me I needed to "get in the trenches with her." For the first time in our relationship, I began to pray for her intentions in a deep way, holding her hand as she dealt with her healing. We would go to the monthly healing Masses at our church, and I would pray hard for her, sometimes next to her as our priest prayed over her. It was during these times I felt most like her protector, forcing me to be the best version of myself. My spiritual armor couldn't protect both of us if there were chinks in it. I started going to daily Mass as often as I could, confession a couple times a month, and began falling in love with Jesus again. If I knew I was going to see her the next day, it motivated me to stay clear of the sin of masturbation, because I wanted to be untainted, clean, and strong during this time she needed me most. And in fighting for her, masturbation and pornography left my life, and I went weeks, then months, free from both leading up to the day of our marriage.

Mimi: After going to a professional Catholic counselor and attending Masses with healing prayers at our parish, I found that our priest was right. I believed, trusted, and surrendered to the love and healing power of our Lord through the ministry of the priesthood. And if you had scratched my family scar on my wedding day, I would have confidently told you that it didn't hurt anymore. I had learned how to forgive in a way I hadn't thought possible.

By the time our wedding day arrived, my experience of

forgiving brought a lot of peace to my heart. I was still feeling some lingering effects of my food addiction, but it was essentially under control. Matt had been free from pornography and masturbation for more than two months before our big day and had been an incredible source of strength for me in our marriage preparation journey. Therefore, I entered into our spiritual and physical marriage covenant feeling great about how far we had both come, and confident that the graces of marriage would take us further into freedom.

Matt: Being free leading up to our marriage was amazing. What I didn't anticipate was that I had to keep fighting impurity even after our wedding. I was dealing with some monumental stresses: a new place to live, a new job, and a new lifelong roommate called a wife. We were also making love, which had awakened a part of my male psyche that I had shut down for months. Working from home gave me a lot of unstructured time, which led me to a lot of undisciplined habits. Then, to my surprise, only a couple weeks after our honeymoon, I succumbed to watching porn.

I felt awful, embarrassed, and guilty. I'm pretty sure I fell after we had made love the night before. "How could this happen?" I wondered. I went to confession that day, but when she got home, she could tell something was different about my demeanor. I knew I couldn't keep this from her if I tried. I sat her down, got down on my knees, and told her what happened that day.

Mimi: The moment Matt confessed to me, everything I knew about addiction, and specifically about pornography, went flying out the window. It was easy for me to understand and forgive before marriage, recalling the struggle with my own addiction. But that was before we had a sexual relationship.

Now, it didn't make any sense.

Ironically, the first thing that came to my mind was not his struggle or insecurity but mine. "Those women are skinnier and prettier than me. My body is fat and ugly, and that's why he doesn't like it." I recognized these lies that I had spent many years redirecting. I combatted these thoughts with my usual positive messages, though they didn't go away so easily this time.

On top of the old lies, I felt new insecurities regarding my willingness and performance in our physical relationship. By the grace of God, I had saved pretty much everything except kissing for when I was married, so our sexual relationship was a new experience for me. Between this and wanting to keep our marital relations pure, there were many things that I was not comfortable with, things that I'd heard through friends or media were expected in the bedroom. Now, all of a sudden, my lack of experience and hesitation in trying new things were a major source of insecurity. "He watched porn because I wouldn't do such and such. He's bored with me already because I won't try anything new. He wouldn't have to watch porn if I would just do or allow some of these things that are expected." The lies infiltrated my head and every part of my being. I was overwhelmed with confusion and sorrow.

Fortunately, these ideas did not come from Matt. On the contrary, he insisted that none of this was the cause of his porn problem. He spoke again and again about how beautiful he found me and repeated the mantras on pornography addiction we both knew so well. I knew he was telling me the truth. I went back to the depths of my own addiction, remembering the times that not even my love for a boyfriend could stop me from bingeing, remembering that the binges and hatred of myself became less and less frequent until they tapered off almost entirely. But, oh, how much harder it was to swallow those facts this time around.

For the first time, in all the years I had known about Matt's use of pornography, I cried. I didn't want to make things worse between us, but in my heart I knew I had to be honest about how I felt. My healing before marriage gave me strength to stand up for myself, so I did not hold anything back. I told him I didn't want to have this conversation ever again, raising the bar to where he was, to what he was finally ready for: total freedom from pornography and not looking back. In addition to my continuing to pray for him, he asked if we could fast together, and it started off as simply giving up chocolate for a month.

After accepting his apology and forgiving him, I had to let it go. To continue to dwell on the doubts would have been an offense to his apology and an impediment to my genuine forgiveness. It would allow his one transgression to continue to affect our marriage because I gave in to the lies about myself. His actions were not due to something I lacked.

Matt: Mimi's forgiving love was saint-like for me. There I was, feeling like I didn't deserve to be loved anymore; but she eventually opened her arms again to me. It was like Jesus loving me, not because of what I do or don't do but for being who I am—including my sins. It humbled me.

I couldn't believe it when I fell again two months later, and continued to fall every two or three months after that for almost a year. We would go through the same process: I would feel awful, she would break down, we would pray and consider what else we could do to fast and pray and take more preventive measures.

Falling over and over didn't come without a cost. Each time I fell, it affected our love life. It was hard at times for Mimi to give fully of herself when she couldn't trust me. Like a saint, however, she would eventually forgive me each time, choose to trust again, and we would move on. She raised the bar higher and higher, and I would go longer and longer between falls.

Mimi: Matt was always awed and humbled by my ability to forgive. But to say, "I had to forgive him and let it go" is to oversimplify my response to each transgression. My development of this Christian ability to forgive and my response to the challenge to continue to practice it didn't end after marriage prep.

In the months following our wedding, I continued to work through the traces and aftereffects of my food addiction. On one retreat, after being prayed over by a priest in front of the Blessed Sacrament, I felt a huge burden lifted through the healing of my heart and mind regarding the addiction and the wound it caused to my self-esteem. By the grace of God, for the first time in my life, I felt peace regarding my eating habits and body. The healing of this wound made it easier for me to accept truth and choose forgiveness in those sporadic times that Matt fell.

The healing of my wound meant accepting how much our Lord loves me, how much he delights in my beauty. To him, I am supremely lovable. His love and affection as my God and creator of my soul meant more to me than any earthly feeling, including the love of my husband.

Because of this, I was able to be more honest with Matt regarding the hurt and disappointment I felt when he fell. Through healing, I allowed the light of the Lord to transform me so that I was more like Christ. In being more like him, I was better able to forgive. It was still a letdown each time Matt fell, but I kept loving him, forgiving him, and expecting him to never fall again.

Matt: Mimi's willingness to love me throughout my falls was a game changer in our marriage. It was this love, when she could have judged me instead, that motivated me most to stay pure. Then, almost a year into our marriage, Mimi went on a four-day pilgrimage to Mexico with some women from our parish. It was during this time, when she was gone having a powerful spiritual experience, that I fell multiple times to porn and masturbation.

This was the lowest of lows for me. Though it's not an excuse, there's something to the fact that the devil was not happy with what was going on in Mexico, and so he picked on me. I felt so guilty when I fell the first time. I just wanted for things to be right again. But, knowing there were more days before she came home, I fell into the temptation of bingeing. The lie in my head was, "Well, she's going to be disappointed with your one fall, you might as well get all the falls in now before she gets back." On the contrary, it was the number of times that I fell that actually upset her the most. I felt so ashamed. How could I do this to her?

When she returned from Mexico, she was ready to be intimate with me but could tell something was off. She was so hurt and broken and angry to find out what I had done while she was gone.

Mimi: Yet again, a new series of angry questions and thoughts came to my head. "Why doesn't he just stop? I keep forgiving him, and he keeps messing up. Maybe I should play tough and deny both forgiveness and sex until he proves he's over this." But in my heart, I knew that wasn't the answer. Only love has the power to overcome any addiction, any sin. He had treated me poorly. It wasn't fair that it put me in such emotional and spiritual turmoil—but I knew I had to forgive him anyway.

Forgiveness is a choice, a deeply Christian choice, to let go of anger toward one who hurt you. Prior to all my spiritual healing experiences, I would have thought forgiveness was neither appropriate nor possible. Now in word and in spirit, I was capable of forgiving. But I was still unsure of the appropriate action. Distrust had been put between us, and I wanted our bond restored. At the same time, I wasn't sure I was ready to give fully of myself and fully welcome him back. While undue anger or revenge wasn't the answer, I needed to be honest with my words and body.

After more prayer and time, I was ready to be open again sexually. But it made me wonder, "How will I feel if he falls again? It's more frustrating every time. Will I ever reach a point where I am unable to forgive?"

And I decided: no. I am determined that I will not be unable to forgive. I am a Christian, I love my God, and he loves me. Christ died for me and has forgiven me of worse transgressions. He has forgiven my husband for his pornography addiction. With every fiber of my being, and with the help of God, I will not let evil win.

Matt: After the Mexico fiasco, Mimi drew it out of me that this addiction could ruin our marriage. It was a wakeup call that motivated me to swallow my pride and take drastic action. I installed pornography filtering software on my laptop and phone and recommitted to praying a daily rosary.

Mimi's unwavering standards and loving forgiveness have helped me tremendously in this fight against the addiction. As many times as I have fallen, not once has she gone easy on me. She always expected me to get back up and never fall again. Her desire to love and be loved melted me, and my motivation has never been fear of her wrath but the desire not to disappoint someone I love. Her consistent choice to love, and her expectation of me to be the man God is calling me to be, have propelled me to another level of freedom. Because Mimi was able to go through her own healing, she has been able to show me that she is a woman worth fighting for, because she is loved by God and knows it. Her Christ-like love in forgiving was part of what made her so beautiful—a beauty I wanted to uphold, protect, and preserve.

Looking back, I realize that the act of sanctifying my wife sanctifies me.

The more she fashions her heart and being after Mother Mary, the more she becomes a woman in Christ's image and likeness, the more evident it is to me how important it is for me to protect and preserve that beauty. If I forget this, if I ever take my eyes off God, it will be no surprise if I fall again.

This idea was clear to me during our engagement, when the finish line of a wedding was very real. In marriage, I've had to learn that fighting for her is a daily choice, and though the end of the battle may not be imminent, it doesn't mean she needs me to fight any less. By the grace of God, the act of masturbation to porn has left our marriage, and the key to staying on this path is the clearest it has ever been.

Mimi: In our story, I've found that addiction recovery is a long process. What I've learned from my own addiction is that the strength to run the last two of a hundred yards to win the victory of being fully healed requires something other than myself. It requires the intense, beautiful, scary, eternal love of Christ. Only Christ can heal the wounds and bring light to the dark places of my soul that not even my husband can reach. In Matt's addiction, I know he needs the same thing.

I can't condone Matt's use of pornography in light of the negative ways it affects our relationship. Yet I know that an angry, bitter, resentful, and unforgiving heart is not going to help him heal. I know I can't judge but have to keep loving and expecting the best. I know I have to believe that this was the last time, that he will not fall again. I know that all of this is possible only if I pray and sacrifice that I may take on the forgiving heart of Christ.

The key to my healing from the hurt Matt's pornography addiction caused was the wholeness of my soul. I had to go back to the past and deal with forgiving a family member. I had to heal from my food addiction and poor body image. It was only through restoration and accepting Christ's immense love for me that I had the courage to accept the truth of our situation and be honest with Matt. It was only through learning how to forgive my family member and myself that I could authentically forgive my husband.

Learning how to forgive allowed me to use love to help Matt break his addiction and ultimately ignite in him the desire to be the man, husband, and eventual father God is calling him to be. It is with these keys that I know that peace, freedom, and purity are possible for both of us.

All Things New

By RACHEL

More than once I've had women say to me, "You don't understand. My story is different. My husband's not just kind of addicted to porn, he views it every day." Or, "It's not just porn and masturbation; he's been sexting with other women, or going to strip clubs." These women feel discouraged when they hear married couples boasting about the healing the Lord has brought about in their marriage. To them, what those couples were facing pales in comparison to what they're up against. If you've had similar thoughts, this next story is for you. Rachel's story is probably the most heart-wrenching one in this book, but it's also incredibly hopeful.

—MATT

Did my husband go looking for pornography, or did pornography find him? That question was answered during our journey together as a young married couple.

In any journey worth taking, there must be a beginning. In his beginning, my husband was born into what some would consider a sexually explosive environment. He kept the story of his childhood hidden from me until long after we were married. Looking back, I think about the day in Seattle where he got down on one knee and proposed to me. Would I have said yes knowing the truth about his early life and how he grew up? Were we even meant to be together at all? Were our three precious, beautiful, intelligent young daughters a complete accident? I like to think Jesus was in control the entire time and that the answers to these questions and the places our journey took us were all a part of his perfect plan.

My husband spent his childhood in a small bedroom community thirty miles from Oklahoma City. His neighbors were simple, working-class folk with young families trying to find their way in the post-Vietnam era of the 1970s. Fifteen hundred miles away in Washington, D.C., the U.S. Supreme Court legalized hardcore pornography in the infamous 1973 case *Miller v. California* when it redefined obscenity from "utterly without socially redeeming value" to lacks "serious literary, artistic, political, or scientific value." I was born the next year. Who could have known that three decades later that court decision would have a lasting impact on my life?

The street where my husband lived had more than its fair share of fatherless homes. Next door lived his best friend, who had a sister who was two years older. She had been introduced to sex at the age of seven. His best friend's mom had been divorced three times. She was a hardworking woman who bartended at night, but her decision to leave her children supervised by a string of her boyfriends left an indelible mark on many of the kids on that street—including my husband.

The first time he laid eyes on pornography was inside that best friend's home around the age of eight. One of the mother's boyfriends kept hundreds of pornographic magazines in a box in the closet. During one of their many sleepovers, the boys snuck into the bedroom, stole a pair of magazines, and raced back to his friend's bedroom.

The first glance was all it took to ignite the tinderbox of curiosity buried deep inside my husband. Whatever innocence he had was snatched away while the boys huddled under a blanket with a flashlight and a magazine as my husband's parents slept peacefully just fifty feet away in the house next door.

Not long afterward, his best friend's sister began looking at the magazines with them. Within a few weeks, their play went from building forts and trading Hot Wheels cars to playing doctor and acting out the scenes depicted in those awful magazines. The three of them had the house to themselves every Friday and Saturday night. As long as they didn't disturb the boyfriend getting stoned in the back bedroom, this new world was theirs to explore.

My husband's parents divorced, and his mom remarried when he was nine. In 1980, my husband's new family moved to a home on two acres in a small town nearby. His access to porn was cut off until a year later when he joined a Boy Scouts troop that was part of the large Southern Baptist church he attended. The scoutmaster was a single man who lived with his mother and sister. The troop had a reputation as an active group that took elaborate trips and went on campouts across the country. My husband loved to travel, so it seemed like a perfect fit.

It turned out the scoutmaster had a collection of pornography that dwarfed the stash at my husband's former neighbor's house. It was the beginning of the VCR age. The scoutmaster had hundreds, maybe thousands, of videos to go along with his boxes and boxes of magazines.

At first, the scoutmaster would have a few of the boys for sleepovers where, inevitably at some point, a porn video would find its way into the VCR. By the time my husband was twelve, the scoutmaster limited the sleepover guests to just my husband and occasionally his brother. The man would set up my husband in the living room with a crate of videos and pretend to say goodnight. My husband watched them all, every single one. There, on a cheap velour couch, amid the smell of homemade cigarettes and dog urine, the stage was set for the battle of a lifetime. He was a child, barely at the onset of puberty, drowning beneath a torrent of pornography being piped into his brain by an adult whom everyone trusted. He was isolated, ashamed, and invisible from the protection of his parents. It was his young will versus the legions of demons who oversee the principalities of the pornography world. It was a battle that would warp his nature and catapult him into oblivion for the next twenty-five years.

Ironically, around the same time, my husband found Jesus. Or did Jesus find him? The large Southern Baptist church that sponsored the scout troop was home to one of the most dynamic youth programs in the nation. In seventh grade, my husband invited Christ to come into his life at summer camp. He was baptized and began to grow as a young disciple. It was almost as if God continued upping the ante every time Satan intensified his attacks. Somehow, by God's grace alone, his life as a young Christian man also began to grow and paralleled his exposure to and immersion in pornography.

The battle raging inside his teenage brain continued into his young adult years. A series of bad dating relationships in college and a distancing from God pushed him to the point where faith was absent from his life. He was heavily into the party scene, had alienated his mother, and rarely stepped foot inside a church for nearly five years after college. He told me these years were like being lost in the dark, convinced he was in a spiritual place not designed for him, all the while knowing deep inside what he really needed was a light to point him in the direction of home.

Things began to change in the spring of 1996. For reasons I still enjoy pondering, God felt I needed a change as well. Our life together began at a teacher's convention in Orlando,

Florida. I was a junior at a small Christian college in South Dakota, and he was a teacher and coach in South Texas.

There was immediate chemistry between us. He could make me laugh out loud without even trying. He claims he liked the way I danced. Perhaps by divine intervention, he rattled off the names of a couple of people with whom he worked who gave him instant credibility with me. His best friends in South Texas had actually grown up with my two older brothers in South Dakota.

I was amazed at the coincidence. The connections gave me comfort knowing that this stranger I had met halfway across the country was someone I could possibly trust. We spent the rest of the conference laughing and dancing and taking long walks together.

He called me at my parents' home the following Sunday. It was Easter morning 1996. I was excited to hear his voice, because when I had boarded the plane to leave Florida, I was almost certain I would never see him again. That summer, he came to visit me and to meet my parents. I visited him a couple of times in South Texas, and all of a sudden, we were a couple. During the teachers' convention in Orlando, he had accepted a teaching job in a tiny native village in southeastern Alaska. He invited me to ride along with him on the drive when he moved there.

At this point, I was in love with him and beginning to think he may be God's chosen mate for me. I decided to make the two week road trip with him up the Alaska Highway to start his new life. We camped and hiked and laughed our way all the way to Tok, Alaska. Every turn in the road was a majestic revealing of God's power and wonder. Everywhere I looked there was another mountain, another glacier, another waterfall, each placed perfectly by God for me to see from the passenger seat of the little 4x4 truck. It was there, during the wildness of that adventure, surrounded by the stunning beauty of the Great Northwest, I heard a whisper deep inside my heart.

In August 1996, my husband flew into Tetlin, Alaska, on a small Piper Cub two-seat plane with just a backpack and a smile. The village of Tetlin is just like what you might see in *National Geographic*, complete with a dirt runway and little barefoot native Alaskan kids surrounding the plane, wondering who this strange white guy was coming to teach them. The village took him in and treated him like family.

I joined him the next fall, after I graduated. Teaching and coaching in Alaska was one of the great joys of my life. We traveled by plane, boat, snowmobile, and dog sled all over Alaska for tournaments and basketball festivals. We went on several world-class hunting and fishing trips with the elders of the village. We loved Alaska, but our personal life that first fall was really, really hard.

Surprisingly, the schools in Alaska are some of the richest in the world, and we had super-fast Internet service in our building, a rarity in 1997. The combination of being isolated with high-speed Internet access and hours upon hours of downtime were the perfect incubator for what would become a devastating and well-hidden pornography addiction for the man whom I now knew I would one day marry.

To start my first year there, we again drove the Alaska Highway, stopping in Seattle to get engaged. A couple of weeks earlier, he had asked my parents for permission to propose to me. I come from a long line of devout German Catholics. He enjoys reminding me that among my eleven aunts and uncles and forty-some cousins, there were no divorces, no crazy people, no outward brokenness. He had longed to have a family like that. He had attended Mass with me several times the previous couple of years and found that it really appealed to him.

We spent the next summer in Juneau while he finished graduate school at the University of Alaska to become a principal. We were married that August on a Saturday, flew to Jamaica on Monday, and were back in Alaska the following Monday. We had accepted new jobs in a larger village north of the Arctic Circle—this time with running water and a grocery store! We were very happy to finally be together.

But his belief that marriage would kill the porn addiction was sadly mistaken. He secretly looked at porn every night after I had gone to bed, telling me he had to be online for graduate school work. He isolated himself and ignored me so that I became depressed and began to loathe our life in Alaska. He handled this like an immature alpha male—by trying to change me and screaming at me to get it together.

What kind of a man looks at porn all night, neglects his wife all day, and then has the audacity to tell her *she* is the one with the problem? I am ashamed to say that I was married to that man for those first five years. I felt so alone, and finally I could not take another second of living that way. I knew I needed to be closer to family and that I was not going to survive in that environment.

In December 1999, we resigned our jobs midyear and moved back to the lower forty-eight. It was a bittersweet good-bye. We had been adopted by the beautiful people of this village. We had discussed starting a family there, maybe even building a house. We had made dear, dear lifelong friends who gave us a traditional Eskimo goodbye celebration and showered us with handmade gifts we still consider to be our most prized possessions.

We told the village that his family had problems and he needed to be closer to them. The painful truth was that the monster of Internet pornography had set its hooks deep into my husband's soul and was running loose in our home, attempting to devour me, our future, and everything in it. I didn't know the monster was just getting warmed up.

When we left Alaska, he got a job as assistant principal at a high school near Kansas City, and I landed a great job teaching special education about five blocks from our apartment. We built a house, joined a thriving parish, were closer to family, and things began to get a little better in our marriage. It was nice to have stores and restaurants and movie theaters nearby. I admit, it was a welcome sight to see the sun for more than a couple hours each day in the winter. Our new home was five hours from both his parents in Oklahoma and mine in South Dakota—walking distance by Alaskan standards.

But once the novelty of our move to warmer weather wore off, I began to sense that the troubles in our marriage ran much deeper than just the isolation I had experienced in Alaska. My husband was still consuming huge amounts of porn (still without my knowledge) and going on drinking trips masquerading as golf outings with the coaches at his school, leaving me at home all the time, alone with our beautiful young daughter.

I married him because I believed he was who God had set aside for me and because I really did love him. He was (and still is) one of the most giving people I have ever met. He has a heart the size of Alaska. His students and most of his teachers loved him because of his unique way of finding the good in almost any crisis. He loves being alive and takes great joy in seeing other people grow and fulfill their God-given potential in life.

But behind all of that stood his pride, casting a shadow over all of the good qualities in him I loved. Fueling his pride was a bottomless appetite for pornography that could have consumed us had God not stepped in.

Around Christmas 2003, he realized he had a serious problem with pornography that was out of control and that he needed professional help. He tells me he remembers getting down on his knees near his "porn altar" in our basement and begging God to help him overcome his addiction. Not long after that, a 5x7 picture of our two-year-old daughter found its way to the shelf above his monitor. I don't recall putting it there, and neither does he. As it turns out, God would be leading this recovery mission.

My husband reached out to his school's social worker, who helped him get into counseling. Meanwhile, he was accepted as a doctoral student at the University of Kansas in February and in March was a finalist to become principal at the school where he had worked for the past four years. He was still looking at porn occasionally, but his usage was down to a couple times a month, well into the "normal" range, which my husband justified. He thought God had miraculously taken the thorn out of his flesh and that he was healed. He was correct that God had begun working in his life and was about to intervene, but not in a way that anyone would have believed.

On April 6, 2004 at about 5:30 a.m., I was eight months pregnant and eating a bowl of cereal in our living room while watching the morning news. A thunderous knock almost caved in our front door and nearly scared me into an early delivery. As soon as I opened the door, I was certain the five federal agents standing on my porch had the wrong house.

They didn't. In 2001, my husband had used his credit card online to get access to some websites that had illicit images of minors. The feds had raided the office of the third-party billing service used by the websites and had the names and addresses of everyone who had purchased monthly memberships. Being an educator, he was in the first wave of people they came after.

They provided a search warrant and took our computers. He told them everything he had done and that he knew he needed help. They interviewed me for more than an hour. I knew absolutely nothing of this evil that had been living in our basement and was working fanatically to destroy the foundation of our lives. I had absolutely no idea he was addicted. I had never seen a single pornographic image in my life. I was in disbelief, shock, terror. All of the above, times a trillion. The federal agents gave me their card, told me to keep an eye on him for fear he might end his life—and simply left the house.

As soon as the door closed, my husband fell to the ground, wailing. I sat motionless. Head in my hands. Totally numb. Too scared to cry. While our two-year-old slept peacefully upstairs, our home had been invaded, our life annihilated. It was our ground zero.

I could write for pages on what the following days, weeks, and months were like, but suffice to say they were pure hell. We were both in physical shock for at least three days. He confesses that he probably would have killed himself had I not been about to deliver our second daughter.

After the agents left and my husband collapsed, he crawled to where I was sitting and begged me not to leave him. He told me bits and pieces of his childhood that were enough for me to hang onto while I began the process of getting my arms around what had just happened.

All the while, God was in control. I am convinced he was in our living room that spring morning. God was there, along with some of his best angels. This was the beginning of his plan, not the end. He loved me and my husband and had been waiting for years to answer a call for help from my husband. I felt his love on me that morning in a way that is indescribable. And then there it was again, that quiet, soft voice coming from way down deep in my heart—"Trust in Jesus . . . just trust in Jesus."

Sometime in those first few days, I sat my husband down and told him I had no intention of leaving him but that he had to get serious help, beginning with seeing a priest. We went together to our parish pastor, who heard our story and his confession. The priest recommended we attend adoration and daily Mass as much as possible and continue to receive intensive marital counseling.

Walking out of church that afternoon, I whispered words to my husband that must have been a message from our guardian angels. I remember saying them but not understanding why at the time: "I love you more right this instant than I ever have before."

Since he was not arrested that first day, and since it was so early in the morning, our neighbors didn't see all of the commotion going on in our home, so we were able to spend the next six months telling our inner circle what he had done. Looking back, I realize that this was just one of several small miracles God would dispense to help us survive what most would consider an un-survivable experience.

It was Holy Week, and my parents came to town on Friday for Easter. I will never forget the sight of my mom getting out of her chair to join him on the floor while he sobbed through the details of what he had done. She hugged him and told him she forgave him and that it was all going to be okay. A few weeks later he told many of his friends on his staff what had happened, including his bosses at the school district. They were all incredibly supportive. He was able to resign his job as a school administrator before the media got involved, and we began to try to prepare for what might lie ahead.

People have often asked me why I didn't just leave then.

Why I didn't take my daughters and go home to my parents? Why would I spend another second in the presence of an accused pedophile? A soon-to-be registered sex offender? Why, one might ask?

The answer is as mysterious as it is simple: Because of Jesus, that's why. Before the creation of the universe, he knew me. He knew my husband. He preordained our life together. None of this makes human sense. It certainly didn't fit anywhere into my plans. This was not the man I married. I didn't know this person was capable of engaging in such behavior.

Believe me, I had my own questions for God. Why couldn't he have used other means to get my husband's attention? Why did it take federal authorities? Search warrants? Why did he have to lose his job that he loved so much and at which he was so good? Why did we have to face public scrutiny and personal humiliation? Why did God use the "nuclear option" on our home, on our innocent girls? Oh, my God, why? As I have come to realize since all this started, I was asking the right Person the wrong question.

Ten months later, in February 2005, my husband pled guilty to one count of possession of child pornography. In May 2005, he was sentenced to thirty-three months in federal prison. In June 2005, I drove him to a low-security prison in northern Minnesota. We shared a long embrace, and he walked inside. By 9 a.m. that hot summer morning, he was in an orange jumpsuit and handcuffs. By 10 a.m., I was parked at a rest area, sobbing hysterically.

He spent the first fourteen days in solitary confinement, where he could not call or write. I went to stay a few days with my parents and prayed so hard for him that a few times I thought I would pass out. Some days later, he was finally allowed to call me, and we cried again together over the phone. He reassured me he was safe and that we could make it through this unimaginable situation. Until then, I had never even been to a jail, never knew anyone who had spent time in jail. Jail was for the worst of the worst, the dregs of society.

That day, dropping him off, I had no intention of taking our girls to see him. We will keep this a secret, I thought. We will hold our breath until he gets home. Military families do it all the time, I told myself. "I am a tough athlete, a South Dakota farm kid. I can do this." Looking back, all those things about me might have been true, but their power could not be claimed until they were whispered again into my ear by our gentle savior.

In prison my husband finally began the process of growing up and becoming an honest man. He spent his time there teaching GED classes, learning Spanish, and serving as the Catholic liaison at the chapel. He got into a program for drug offenders and throughout the courses substituted "porn ad-diction" any time he saw the word "drugs" or "alcohol." He became healthy in every area of his life.

We wrote love letters to each other every day. We did a couple of book shares, including *The 5 Love Languages* by Gary Chapman, a must-read for all couples. We learned to share our feelings in the eight minutes of phone time we had per day. Ironically, I reflect fondly on these months—not be-cause we were separated, but because we were communicat-ing and relying on each other and on God to get us through each day.

Once I learned prisons are nothing like what we see on *Lockup*, I drove nine hours one way to visit him nineteen times while he was there. I brought the kids on ten of those trips, several times in the dead of winter. They were two and three at the time and just happy to be going to see Daddy "at work."

While he was gone, life was surprisingly good and simple. We had enough money set aside that, with the help of some close friends and family, we could keep our house, and I could stay home with our girls and not have to work. I focused all of my energy on them, and did all I could to shield them from the loss of their father. Some of the teachers at his former school adopted our girls and made sure they were loved to the point the kids believed these people were part of our family (which they are).

Many of his closest friends, including several from his teaching staff along with a few students, went to visit him in prison, each of them angels in their own unique way. We fully experienced the trueness of the proverb that claims we learn who our real friends are by how they treat us during our time of most desperate need.

In February 2007, when my husband had about nine months left to serve, his prison counselor told him a clerical mistake had him in the wrong drug program and that he actually qualified for an early release opportunity. Seven days later, on St. Valentine's Day, I picked him up and drove him back home to Kansas.

That was a Wednesday. The next Sunday, we had a family reunion to celebrate the end of this wrenching three-year experience. We attended Mass in Leavenworth, Kansas, near the halfway house to which he was assigned. That Sunday, instead of giving a homily, the priest showed a video on pornography addiction prepared by the archdiocese. Unbelievable! We were all in tears by the end of the video and were sure we had just been part of an obvious miracle. God had reached down into that prison and plucked him out so that our family could see that video together in that moment, under those circumstances! We knew right then and there that God would receive the glory through our suffering.

We wrote our archbishop a letter the next day offering to do whatever he thought we could to help with this epidemic.

Unfortunately, my husband had much more work to do before God would consider him suitable for battle in this arena.

My husband was on federal probation for two years. The authorities placed monitoring software on our laptop, and he had to attend weekly classes for men who had committed similar offenses. To "graduate" from this program, he had to pass a series of polygraph tests verifying he had not viewed any pornography while he was on probation.

Up to this point, my entire battle had been with the legal system, the courts, the prison, and all the things that go along with that. I hadn't given myself permission to focus on his addiction, on pornography, and what actually had led us to this point in our journey. Perhaps I was too scared of the answers I would find. Yet again, God was in control and had plans to introduce me, in his good time, to the real face of this addiction.

In the fall of 2009, my husband relapsed. No more than two months after the monitoring software was removed from our laptop, I opened his Internet history and found he had been surfing porn again.

"Oh, dear God," I thought. "Not again!" "How could he?" "After what we just survived?" "You bastard!" Until that instant, I had never in my life laid eyes on a single pornographic image. The Web pages he had visited played before me as I sat crying at his desk. If his first arrow had wounded me, this surely was the kill shot.

I raced upstairs with the laptop, kicked open the door, and threw it on top of him as he slept. I exploded with fury this time. I trembled as the words spewed out of me like an unstable volcano. I screamed at him until my throat hurt, my last words being "Just get out!" He walked past me on his way to sleep in his truck.

All of a sudden, the words I had heard at our church VIR-

TUS training came gushing out of my memory. Men with this addiction are incurable! The recovery rate is less than five percent. What man, who after losing his entire career and nearly his family, would dare go there again? My God, is he even capable of changing? What the hell am I doing here?

For the first time, I began entertaining the idea of leaving him. I prayed to God to give me an answer. "Stay and fight?" "Leave and start over?" His answer would come to me clear as a bell—and yet in a whisper.

Since he couldn't go back to education, we had decided to use some of the business plans we had written while in prison to start a new life. We started cleaning houses together, then churches and small offices. Pretty much anything someone would pay us to do, we did. After attorney's fees, fines, and two years without income, we were bankrupt and had no savings left. We worked hard and lived hand-to-mouth for several months.

I became pregnant with our third child, and one day God decided to add to that miracle by blessing our small business. One of my closest friends, who had been at my side since ground zero, worked at a large office building. She put in a good word for us with its facility manager and we landed our first large cleaning contract. It allowed us to hire a full-time employee so we could focus on selling and growing the business. God continued to bless us, and we ventured into other things like landscaping and snow removal. Now, by God's grace alone, we have about eight full-time employees and are doing just fine.

After being exposed the second time, my husband knew he was out of chances with me. During his pretrial stage, he had gone to a psychiatrist who had conducted a thorough battery of psychosexual tests on him. The results were clear that although he was a very low risk to harm anyone, he had a clinical addiction to pornography and that to hope for any chance at recovery, he would have to reorganize his entire life and deal openly with his addiction.

I set some hard ground rules for him if we were to continue as a couple. We immediately put pornography filtering software on our home computer. He was not to use any device without some kind of porn-blocking software. We also began to seek the counsel of a family therapist who specialized in the area of sexual addiction. While my heart was broken into a jillion pieces all over again, my brain told me there was more to this issue than what I was seeing in my husband.

As I mentioned earlier, about the time he was released from prison, our archdiocese launched a new program for men and families struggling with sexual addiction called the My House Program. A bright young therapist was hired to lead the program, and he established weekly men's recovery groups at various parishes all over town.

My husband began attending a group that fall and has been going ever since. It took a while for him to find the recovery model that fit his needs, but he now meets regularly with three other men who struggle with the same issue. They are working through a twelve-step recovery program centered on the Theology of the Body material written by Pope St. John Paul II and condensed by Christopher West.

Around this time, I realized that, if the marriage was to continue, I would need intensive therapy to heal my own pain. Although my husband was the one who had pierced my heart, I felt it was up to me to remove the arrow. Any time a person has been injured or wounded, it is up to the victim to take charge of his recovery—to seek the help of a doctor, to take the medicine, and to care for his own wound.

This is a vitally important concept for any woman who

has been hurt by the deeds of others. It is impossible for the perpetrator to fix us, to heal us, or to save us. Imagine if you were in a car wreck that broke your ankle and that it wasn't your fault. Once the guilty driver's insurance paid for your repairs and your medical bills, it is clearly your responsibility to take it from there. Would you ever ask the driver of the car who hit you to decide where you bought your new car, to pick out the color, or to remind you to go to your physical therapy appointments?

We must take control of our own healing! We have to choose wellness over brokenness. Protect ourselves and set clear boundaries on those who have hurt us? Absolutely! But after the knife has been removed from our backs, it is our choices that grant us access to the restorative, healing grace God has waiting.

A couple of years later, I attended a conference called Women of Virtue. I had the privilege of hearing Doug Weiss speak about the brain science behind intense pornography addiction. He spoke of other couples who had endured the same—and even worse—trauma as had I and said that healing, recovery, and renewal were happening every day across the country.

I began reading everything I could on pornography addiction and noticed a common thread in all the stories. They all sounded the same: it was usually smart, hardworking, regular men just like my husband; all good fathers, husbands, soccer coaches, bankers, teachers, and guys from all walks of life. They were falling en masse to this terrible addiction.

For the first time, I began to consider the possibility that his relapse was not a conscious choice he made, but a byproduct of the years and years of brain conditioning he had self-inflicted as he sat staring at the images on the monitor. I learned about dopamine, oxytocin, Delta PhosB, and all the chemicals God embedded in our brains as part of his perfect plan for our sexuality. I saw CAT scans and learned how the porn-addicted brain is identical to the heroine-addicted brain. I learned that when manipulated with an intense stimulus like pornography, the chemical reactions in our brains produce addictions easily as powerful as addictions to nicotine, cocaine, and heroin. Most importantly, I learned that the lives of men with full-blown pornography addictions are as unmanageable as those of anyone battling dependency on powerful narcotics to manage their pain.

At the Women of Virtue conference the next year, I met Christopher West and heard him eloquently portray the Theology of the Body works written by Pope St. John Paul II. I heard him tell of all of the brokenness that exists in our world as a result of disordered sexuality.

That night, leaving the church, my husband and I reflected on our journey together. His miraculous early release from prison so we could see that video was too much of a coincidence. We knew that with God, and through the Holy Spirit, there are no coincidences. We were being called to speak out, to tell our story and to use our experience however the Father saw fit to draw attention to this terrible problem. Possibly even to bring hope to other couples who may be facing the same monsters in their homes.

Since attending these conferences, as the years pass by my husband and I have been growing again as a couple. He is on step nine of his twelve-step recovery journey, and I still monitor all of his electronic devices. He works hard to be a great father to our three gorgeous girls. In return, they love him madly.

Ten years to the day the police came to our house with a search warrant, we purchased the domain name KingDavids-Rock.org. We are in the process of selling our company with plans to transition into establishing a fundraising mechanism to support education about, prevention of, and recovery from Internet pornography addiction in our community. There are probably more questions than answers on that front, but we have dropped our nets and are turning to follow Jesus.

Anyone reading this may call me naïve. I am sure some in my life have even whispered how weak or unhealthy I must be for forgiving my husband twice and choosing to stay married to him. I disagree. Jesus calls us to forgive others not just seven times but seventy times seven times. I forgive my husband daily for all kinds of things, as he does for me, as all couples have to do. Forgiving my husband and inviting Jesus into our home to guide our marriage is not enabling anybody. Rather, it is empowering God to use our brokenness for his glory.

Am I restored? I can say with certainty that being restored is not a single event we mark on a calendar to which we point and say, "Yep, there it is, that's the day he fixed me." Renewal is a daily choice we make each morning when we open our eyes and ask Jesus to help us lead our best life possible. Somehow, that usually begins with a measure of forgiveness.

I was restored the day I was baptized into the Church and again on the day of my First Communion. I get restored every Sunday during Holy Communion and in the quiet of the night while in the presence of the Blessed Sacrament inside our adoration chapel. I feel restored when I see my girls playing with their Daddy in our living room, when I hear them laughing, and I smile, knowing our family journey is just beginning. I am restored when I pause during the craziness of my busy life to realize how my choice to stay and fight is the only thing that shields our little girls from the brokenness and pain of divorce. It is a choice I embrace. Thank you, Jesus, for restoring me again today.

The Road to Recovery

By POLLY

One helpful way to understand the allure of pornography is to think of it as an escape behavior—a very efficient way to escape the pain, frustration, and tedium of daily life. When one has learned to do this from an early age, as many men have (the average age a boy is exposed to pornography today is twelve), it can stunt his emotional maturity, his ability to cope with difficult or disappointing situations. When he gets stressed out, his body knows exactly where to go to feel better. Polly describes how this was the case with her husband. When things were going well, he was the perfect friend and husband. When something irritated him, he'd explode. Once Jake began to find freedom from pornography, he then had to embark upon the long journey of processing his pain without escaping to pornography.

—MATT

If you're like me, you've had a time in your life when you wanted to be loved so desperately it hurt. At the same time, like me, you felt deep down that you'd never be worthy of kind, honest love.

I spent much of my single life like that; aching for someone to know me and love me, yet constantly feeling abandoned by the men who kissed me and then never called again. And it figured. *I'll only ever be loved a little because I'm only a little bit loveable.*

Sick of suffering from depression and anxiety, I started a whole-hearted search to learn the skill of happiness—with or without romantic love. I searched Scripture and prayed. God couldn't have sent us down here to be miserable, right? Didn't he send us to learn to have peace and joy in spite of trials?

In Luke 10:27, we discover that we must love God with our whole heart, soul, strength, and mind. And that we must love our neighbor as ourselves.

Developing a healthy love for yourself isn't easy, especially after you've been searching for someone else to do it for you. I began therapy, did yoga, and started meditating. I looked at myself in the mirror and said, "I love you." I started feeling the love of God as I stopped putting myself down and being desperate for love from others.

Around this time, I found a poem that changed my life:

Love After Love

The time will come
when, with elation
you will greet yourself arriving
at your own door, in your own mirror
and each will smile at the other's welcome,

and say, sit here. Eat.
You will love again the stranger who was your self.
Give wine. Give bread. Give back your heart
to itself, to the stranger who has loved you
all your life, whom you ignored

for another, who knows you by heart.
Take down the love letters from the bookshelf,

the photographs, the desperate notes,
peel your own image from the mirror.
Sit. Feast on your life.

—*Derek Walcott*

Inspired by this poem, I learned to love myself. I learned to
care for myself. I learned to set healthy boundaries. I learned
the skill of happiness. It took years.

I found that I could love others more. I had more compassion for the weaknesses of others, more patience.

Knowing that I am a daughter of God, and by default worthy of being loved and cherished, I started to break up with
men who didn't adore me (which was every one). But I was
okay with that. I could ask for and expect a whole-hearted
relationship. I came to believe that I could find a partner who
would love me freely, with a kind, pure heart. And I actively
began seeking that type of person.

Then I met Jake. Within days of meeting online, we talked
on the phone. Immediately we both felt a connection. Having
a concrete sense of what I wanted, I finally had the courage
to say, "I really like you. I'm only interested in continuing to
talk if you're serious about having a relationship. I'd like you
to call me every day at 9 p.m."

He didn't push back. In fact, he was excited. He said, "Are
you my phone girlfriend?"

I said, "Yes, we're exclusively phoning."

Three months later, we traveled the long distance to meet
in person, and our connection grew and grew. I set boundaries early on. One of my boundaries was no porn. I told him

that I would not tolerate my boyfriend using porn or mastur-bating, and he readily agreed.

In that moment, he lied. And then, the next two years were built on that lie. He had been habitually masturbating for years, and thought that marriage would solve his problem.

We got engaged, and most of our engagement was a beau-tiful, exciting time. But about once a week, he would lash out at me about something small. I saw the red flag, and I told him he would have to get therapy for his anger once we got mar-ried. But I, too, had the mistaken idea that sex would help. In fact, his family witnessed one of the times he lashed out at me, and his mom said, "It's just because you can't have sex. Once you can have sex, he won't be like that anymore."

When marriage didn't solve all his sinful problems, like he thought it would, he blamed me—though not to my face. He was lying constantly by this time: lying to cover up the first lie and to continue hiding his behavior. But as he blamed me from inside his own head, he became increasingly irritable and angry. We fought about everything.

One day, I made cookies for the neighbors. He came home from work and smelled the cookies, but couldn't find any. I said, "I took the cookies to the neighbors."

He said, "What?! How could you? Do you not have any respect or love for me? What kind of wife does that to her husband?"

I said, "There's cookie dough in the fridge. Would you like me to bake some for you now? It'll take ten minutes."

"If you cared for me at all, these cookies would be sitting on the table for me right when I get home. It's too late now; I know how you really are."

This type of dialogue happened over just about everything. I soon realized I was living with Jekyll *and* Hyde. Eighty per-cent of the time, Jake was loving and kind and helpful and funny. The rest of the time he was cruel, illogical, and emotionally abusive.

I said, "Jake, I love you. Something isn't right. You're an amazing husband most of the time, but then what happens to you? Where does my loving husband go? The man who is supposed to love and cherish me would not treat me like this. If you don't go to therapy, I'm leaving."

He started therapy, but because he didn't tell the truth about the pornography and masturbation, it didn't do much. I constantly asked him if he was looking at porn or masturbating, because I knew that sex addicts lie and have mental health issues. But pornography is almost impossible to detect. If someone is lying to you, there's not much you can do to catch him. So, I just focused on his abusive behavior.

There were times when I went back to my depressed self— *of course this would happen to me, it always does* type of self-talk. I felt sad. I had waited so long to find the man of my dreams, and here I was again, feeling emotionally abandoned and attacked by the man who was supposed to protect me. Even after my son was born I would sometimes think to myself, *No one will ever really love me.*

But then, that poem would come into my mind, and I would say, "I love you, Polly. I'll take care of you. You're going to be okay." And I would feel God's love for me through my continued prayers, study, and the peace that came from keeping his commandments.

Throughout all this, I reached out to my family and friends. I told them about what was happening. I told them I was scared.

One night, as I held our baby, my husband screamed, "I HATE YOU!"

I asked Jake to leave the house. I knelt by our bed and prayed for help. I prayed for the safety of my husband because

I thought he was on his way to commit suicide. I prayed to know what to do. After my prayer, I called my dad. He was calm. He said, "Do you want to get divorced?"

I said, "I don't know. I don't know what to do."

"Whatever you decide, we love you and we'll support you," he said.

Things got gradually worse. Due to the economic downturn in 2009, we both lost our jobs. We had to sell our house at a loss. I was living in limbo, not knowing how to move forward; frozen. Futilely I tried to confront Jake, almost on a daily basis, about why he was so emotionally immature and illogical.

I think my recovery from depression before our marriage helped me be strong and stand up to him. The more he raged, the more I recognized that he was not emotionally healthy and he needed help. However, the more I tried to help, the more he perceived me as his enemy.

But guess what? I'm still married to Jake. And I love him more than anything. And I feel more loved and cherished than I have ever felt. I have a healthy marriage with the man of my dreams.

Eighteen months into our marriage, after I had asked him almost weekly if he had a porn and masturbation problem, Jake told the truth.

Here is how it happened. After we lost our jobs and sold our house we packed up and moved 700 miles away into my parent's basement. Because we had an infant I had to care for, Jake packed up our home by himself.

During this time, he was using pornography and masturbation to deal with the stress of his failure. He had failed as a provider, failed as a husband, failed as a father—or at least that's how he saw it.

One morning, he woke up and went to turn on the computer again. But instead, he knelt in prayer. In that prayer, God gave him a vision of what his life would be like if he didn't stop his compulsive behavior—it would destroy him, his wife, and his infant son. Whether he stayed in the marriage and told me the truth or left the marriage, if he didn't change we all would be utterly decimated.

He realized he needed to recover from the addiction regardless of the outcome of our marriage, and knew I would likely leave him. But he committed to tell the truth regardless. He wanted recovery for himself.

Jake didn't come home when he said he would. I could sense something wasn't right. When an addict decides to change, it doesn't happen overnight. He's an addict because he's emotionally immature, and stopping the compulsive behavior doesn't change that fact.

Jake packed all our stuff into a storage unit, not knowing what would happen to us, and started the twelve-hour drive to my parents. That night he stayed at a nasty little hotel.

Back at my parents', a wave of dread came over me. I knew something was wrong. I was terrified that he had solicited a prostitute or that he would attempt suicide. I prayed for his life and for his soul.

I could not reach Jake on his phone. I tried calling the hotel, but it didn't have a phone in the room. I panicked.

That night in the hotel, not having emotional skills to deal with negative emotions in healthy ways, he tried to numb himself by drinking alcohol—though he had never had so much as a drop in his entire life.

Later, he told me that he realized that he was about to trade one addiction for another, and poured the rest of the alcohol down the sink. He said he was wracked with the torment of hell that night, not having anything to numb the pain, having to feel the full weight of his choices.

The next morning, I called and called, but he didn't answer the phone. I feared he was dead.

When he finally called me around 11 a.m., he said he'd been eating breakfast.

"You are avoiding coming home," I said.

He said, "No, I'm not."

"You have an eight-hour drive, and it's eleven and you haven't started. That's not the behavior of someone who wants to get home. You'd be halfway home by now if you wanted to come home. Something is wrong. Have you been looking at pornography?"

"Yes."

"Have you been masturbating?"

"Yes."

And in that short conversation, all my suspicions were realized. I wasn't crazy. There was a very real reason for his anger and irritability and it sure wasn't because I hadn't made him cookies. I said, "We'll talk about it when you get home."

Wives of sex addicts often agree that the lying and the emotional drama that taint the day-to-day moments is the worst part. Women married to men who watch porn don't have loving, peaceful marriages. The marriage is riddled with drama, lying, blaming, isolating behaviors, anger, and criticism. This is why women hate porn: it ruins men.

I waited at my parents, wringing my hands. I told my mom that I was worried. I prayed and prayed, read the Bible and prayed more. He should have been home around seven or eight. He didn't come home. And he didn't come home. And he wasn't answering his phone. My dread intensified.

Finally, shortly before midnight, he came in. I was so angry and terrified, yet relieved he wasn't dead. I said, "We'll have a lot to talk about tomorrow." And I went to bed.

But in the morning, he acted like nothing had happened. I felt so stupid for believing him. So I came out guns blazing, knowing we had a long haul ahead of us if we were going to survive. I didn't hold anything back.

He didn't seem especially remorseful, just empty and numb. He had tried for so long to avoid the pain of hearing how much pain he had caused, but all his efforts didn't work. I said, "You can be angry all you want. But I'm going to get help by telling people about what's going on."

(Soon after, Jake started therapy and started working the Twelve Steps. He started a blog to document his recovery, and if you want to read more about it, visit recoverywithjake.org. But this isn't his story. This is my story.)

For the first two years of recovery, he was still Jekyll and Hyde. People watch porn to numb themselves from negative emotions. When you take away their coping mechanism, they are left with nothing—and feeling negative emotions with no healthy way of dealing with them is excruciating.

So although Jake had stopped the porn and masturbation, he wasn't emotionally healthy instantly. He was feeling the full weight of agonizing emotions for the first time. It was just Jake and his negative emotions, with nothing in between. This time was very painful for him and for me as he learned to cope with his negative emotions in healthy ways—rather than isolate with porn. At times, he couldn't muster any compassion for me. He had to learn the skill of emotional connection.

Many wives are afraid to face the truth of their situation. My hope is that, through prayer, women can muster the faith and strength to face the truth. And the truth will set them free.

Before Jake learned the skill of emotional connection and dealing with negative emotions in healthy ways, I had to take an objective look at the situation. It was difficult to sort through the mess to see the truth. So, I started looking for facts. What was the reality of my situation?

Fact 1: I refused to be isolated from friends and family.
After one of Jake's anger episodes, I called all my friends in my apartment complex. I told them what happened and I told them I needed support. Then I ordered a bunch of pizza and had a pizza party at our pool. When Jake got home, he came to the party. At the party, he said he was sorry. He didn't rage about the party or the pizza. He told me it was a good idea to get support. Any time I did something like this, he supported me—even though he felt stupid.

The fact that I continued to reach out to people and to speak the truth about my situation helped me move forward in our marriage, knowing that I wasn't living a double life. I was honest with myself and others, and that brought me peace.

It also helped Jake heal because he knew I wouldn't be making excuses for his behavior or enabling him in any way. He had committed to being honest at that point as well, and transparency is really the beginning of true healing. Because honesty is the highest form of intimacy, we were able to start connecting in ways not possible before.

Fact 2: I could determine the truth of my situation if I tracked our fights.
I started tracking Jake's behavior—literally. On a calendar I would write, "Jake yelled at our son and me today about our son's new pants." I could see, in factual terms, that he was angry and irritable about three days out of every thirty. The monster in Jake would come out only ten percent of the time.

I've found that the root of addiction is emotional immaturity, the tendency to isolate and numb when feeling negative emotions, rather than turn to God or others and connect. As he recovered, I continued to track, and I could see literal, statistical progress. We're now at five minutes of rage every six months. Not bad, right? And it's getting better every day.

Fact 3: I could do whatever I needed to do.

Many women I talk to say, "I can't talk to my husband about porn; he'll get mad." That, my friends, is playing the victim. In spite of Jake getting outraged, I said my peace. I told him exactly what I was thinking and what I expected: love, compassion, understanding. I held my ground as he raged. And I didn't rage back. I felt like a dandelion, swaying from the hot breath of an angry dragon. But, I stood tall, and faced it, without swearing or yelling or demeaning him. And then I said, "That is not true. These are the seven reasons why you are not making any sense." That would generally make him more angry, but I never backed down.

I stayed because I could trust myself. I knew that I could say what needed to be said, no matter how painful and scary. And I knew I could see the truth of the situation, in spite of his attempts to manipulate me or turn things around.

Fact 4: I could ask my husband to do things and then observe his behavior.

Many wives of addicts stop requesting things of their husbands, like taking out the trash or family prayer, because they're afraid. I was afraid, too. For example, I was afraid to ask him to get up with our son at night because he might turn it around like he had before and say, "You don't support my career." But I asked him anyway, in spite of my fears.

I asked Jake to read the Bible. I asked him to fast to learn what God wanted him to do in order to heal. I asked him to do many things.

Jake stepped up. He listened to my requests and said, "Yes. In order to build trust with you again, I will do that."

Sometimes, when he didn't know how to deal with his negative emotions, instead of raging against me, he would silently do the dishes, fold laundry, and take our kids for a walk. He started to do productive things to help our family when he felt stress or pain, instead of isolating into work or porn or video games.

As I observed his behavior, I started to consider trusting again.

Fact 5: I could educate myself.

Did you know that there are support groups for wives of sex addicts? For example, I joined TogethernessProject.org and BloomforWomen.com. I started learning about what addict behavior looks like and what recovery behavior looks like.

With education, everything becomes very clear. It was nice to know that I wasn't alone and that the behaviors I observed were common to sex addicts. It helped me separate out Jake's true character from the addiction.

Fact 6: Working with what I had was better than starting over.

When Jake finally told me the truth about his pornography and masturbation, I was relieved because I knew the truth.

However, because I thought our entire marriage was based on a lie, I really wanted to get a divorce. When I called the attorney, I asked him if there was any way I could never, ever see Jake again. The attorney said that I would always have to interact with Jake because we had a son together. I realized that Jake was in my life forever, no matter what. Either I stayed married to him, or I would see him every week as we exchanged our son. I was so angry. I wanted to be rid of him forever. In that moment, I decided that if I had to see Jake for the rest of my life regardless, the best-case scenario was a happy, loving marriage. Believing that people can change, I decided to see if he *would* change.

Changing meant more than just stopping the porn. Jake had to learn to be emotionally mature, and that took years, even after he stopped the compulsive sexual behavior.

Fact 7: I could choose to trust again when I felt safe.

We are commanded to forgive because it helps us be happy and feel peace—we connect with others when we forgive.

But we are not commanded to trust. Trusting someone who's not trustworthy is harmful.

Despite my anger, the forgiveness came easy with Jake. I didn't want to hurt myself (Jake had already done that), so forgiveness was almost instantaneous. I didn't want to hold myself back and punish myself. I needed peace.

The trust is an entirely different issue. It's really not a good idea to trust someone who has lied to you and abused you for years.

I believe that Christ can change people—literally make them a new person, with new habits and ways of dealing with life. But Christ will only change people if they work to be changed. I trust Christ and I trust the process of repentance.

I have to trust my gut. I watch Jake's behavior to know if we're connecting, or if he's isolating. We're still working through this. Sometimes I'm scared. I have flashbacks of the abusive episodes. I tell Jake about this, and he comforts me now, and feels the pain I'm going through. We are still in therapy to help me heal from the trauma.

Because he reacts this way, it helps me choose to trust him. And I choose to trust him because his behavior warrants my trust.

**Fact 8: I believed that Christ could change Jake, and I
had faith in the process.**
Watching someone change takes patience. I watched as Jake
worked through the twelve steps. It took him two years to
genuinely and authentically accomplish the steps, but along
the way, he realized that the twelve steps are not a checklist.
They're a lifestyle.

I saw steady progress in Jake's ability to connect, to take
responsibility for his own actions, to stop blaming me, to stop
raging at others when he was feeling stressed.

Many wives go through a period of feeling like they're crazy. The lying, blaming, and emotional abuse that often accom-
pany sex addiction are the most difficult parts to heal from in
a marriage. Stopping the behavior is just the first step to recovering from addiction. To really recover, you must learn to
connect and be emotionally healthy. I frequently wonder how
many people suffer from mental disturbances and emotional
immaturity because of their pornography use, but because
they're unwilling to admit that they use, or they discount
porn as something everyone does, they suffer needlessly, and
hurt their loved ones in the process.

I'm so grateful and proud of Jake for his progress. For taking responsibility. I'm proud of him for learning the skills of
connection and happy emotional choices.

And I'm proud of myself for knowing that God loves me
and wants me to have a beautiful, happy marriage. It takes
work, but when you know something is possible, it's worth
the effort.

The Story I Never Thought I Would Tell

By ANNE

I remember seeing an ad that showed two pictures: one of a boy and one of a man. The ad was about child abuse, and it said something like, "It's easy to have compassion for one (the boy) and to hate the other (the man) . . . until you realize they're the same person." At this point the two photos came together showing that the boy who had been abused ended up becoming an abuser. Something similar might be said of the porn addict. It's easy to have compassion on the boy who is sexually abused, or who is exposed to pornography, and to feel nothing but resentment and disgust at the man who is a porn addict . . . until you realize they're the same person. Now, I'm not saying this makes a man's porn use (or child abuse, for that matter) justifiable; of course it doesn't. But it should help us to have compassion for the person in question. None of us asked to be born into this pornified culture, but here we are. Let us pray that we may have compassion on ourselves and those who have hurt us most.

—MATT

There are days when I would trade all of this in a heartbeat for something less messy and traumatic. There are other days when I am truly amazed at what Jesus is doing and how he is present through it all. It isn't easy to expose myself and my husband in such a raw way for others to look inside our life, but I know there are many women who want to speak up but feel they can't.

I had a Norman Rockwell upbringing, with wonderful, loving parents and a family in which I felt safe and protected. I loved being around them, even when we were loud and got on each other's nerves. I experienced no real trauma in my family of origin. As I got older, I learned what pornography and masturbation were but never heard them talked about at home or at our local school or parish. I never heard the phrase "sex addict," and it never dawned on me that there were such people in the world.

I met my husband, Paul, at a local Catholic young adult group. I remember seeing him walk in the door for the first time and thinking how handsome he was. We were introduced and made small talk over some chocolate chip cookies. Over the summer, we began to hang out more; we went on a young adult retreat, saw each other at praise-and-worship nights, and began swing dancing together. By fall, he asked me for permission to start dating.

What I loved most about Paul was his love of the Catholic Faith. As I grew in my faith, marrying a man who sought the heart of Jesus was at the top of my list. Paul loved Jesus and his faith; he was smart and could articulate philosophy and theology. He loved God, and he loved me. What more could a girl want?

Though we did not have sex before marriage, being chaste was a constant struggle for us. Looking back, I can see how that struggle encouraged my husband's acting out and his hiding it from me (and even from himself, to a degree) during our dating and courtship.

At the time, Paul told me he struggled with masturbation. I did not fully understand what that entailed. He told me about his struggles: how he felt guilt and shame, and how he tried to pray away temptation and stay strong with the grace of the sacraments. I tried to be loving and encouraging but had no idea what his struggle really meant or how it would affect our relationship. After ten months of dating, we became engaged in August 2011.

One night, we were hanging out at my parent's house and Paul told me he had recently masturbated. It felt like a ton of bricks had come crashing down on me. I remember bursting into tears and crying so hard and he held me to try and calm me down. He had a blank look on his face. He was so ashamed and incapable of knowing how to talk about this with me.

So what happened after that? Nothing. We did not discuss the issue any further. There was no talk of this being a problem—dare I say an addiction. I didn't ask questions (maybe because I was too scared to hear the answers), and Paul didn't want to talk about it. Even after this, I never had an inkling that my husband was a sex addict, and this incident never placed a doubt in my mind about marrying this man. At the time, I had no idea how consumed he was with this disease; how it twisted everything—from how he saw himself as a man to his views of sex and intimacy. Even in our marriage preparation, these issues never came up; certainly there was no discussion of the devastating effects sexual addiction has on a marriage.

We married on a beautiful summer day in June 2012. The next day we flew to Seattle to go on an Alaskan cruise for our honeymoon. It all seemed so perfect, like a storybook ending in a Disney movie. I can remember looking back at the moment we exchanged vows and realizing the great seriousness of the promise we made to each other and to God. I meant those words to the core of my being, and I think Paul did as well—as much as he was capable of. But neither of us imagined how those vows would be tested early in our marriage. I was very innocent when we got married. Paul was blind to the fact he had an addiction and he thought these problems would disappear after marriage.

Fast-forward seven months to right after the new year. Paul walked in the door from an appointment for spiritual direction. I knew instantly that something was terribly wrong. It was all over his face. Paul asked me to sit down and said he needed to tell me something. My husband of seven months told me he had been smoking marijuana with a medical license for several months *and* that he had been having a difficult time being on the computer so much for grad school; he struggled with viewing pornography and masturbating.

In that moment, I felt my world utterly destroyed. The dreams I had for my marriage were swept away by just a few sentences. To say I was in shock would be a gross understatement. I felt sick to my stomach and numb.

The following months were the darkest I have ever experienced. Paul and I barely spoke; when we did, he raged or I cried hysterically to the point of becoming physically ill. I wanted the pain to stop. I wanted it all to go away. I wanted to wake up from the nightmare. I felt like a zombie walking through a heavy fog.

At my darkest times, I thought of hurting myself or taking my own life. I had frequent nightmares (and still do) of Paul acting out sexually. I even imagined what it would be like to kill my husband. I wanted Paul to suffer for the trauma he caused me and our marriage. I just wanted all the pain to go away. I felt utterly hopeless. Married not even a year, I wanted to run away and leave my husband. I began to think seriously that I had grounds for an annulment.

Amid the darkness, I was, and am, continually blessed to have the loving support of my family, close friends, and the wives in the support group I attend. My parents and my sister knew about what was going on in our marriage. I didn't really give Paul an option. I told him I needed to confide in the people I loved the most. I needed someone to talk to, or I thought I might lose my mind.

Although some would say it's crazy to tell your parents about your husband's sexual addiction, for me it was, and continues to be, a healthy, safe refuge where I can be honest and not be judged. Their love and prayers have been an indispensable comfort as Paul and I struggle through this. I cannot imagine facing this problem without Mom and Dad listening, praying, and supporting me.

The recovery process for my husband and me has been painstakingly slow. After Paul's disclosure, we began marriage counseling. That spring, Paul started attending a support group at a local parish for men who struggle with sex addiction. He discovered there was a similar group for wives. The pain of having to attend this group was second only to learning about my husband's addiction.

Though I knew I needed to be there, in the beginning I just sat and cried and cried. It was awful. I hated the fact I needed to go; that I was one of "those" women—the wife of a sex addict. Each week it felt like I was ripping the bandage off a wound over and over again, and each time the pain again oozed out.

In time, I cried less at the meetings and began to learn from these amazing women. I began to see that I couldn't go just because of my husband—I needed to be there for me, for

Anne. I needed to work through my own feelings and heal from the trauma all this had caused. It is still today one of the safest, most loving, and supportive communities I have ever been a part of. Some of the women I look up to and admire most are the wives in this group.

Nearly a year later, right before Christmas, my husband was arrested for drunk driving. After that awful incident, Paul began to see a certified sex addiction therapist and was able to acknowledge that although he was not a drug addict or an alcoholic, acting out with substances was a way to distract himself from his primary addiction, which was sexual.

Three months after the DUI, I sought out a therapist who specialized in dealing with spouses who are married to sex addicts. Even with both of us seeing therapists and going to our support groups, life often felt like an unsafe rollercoaster; and I just wanted the ride to stop. Paul struggled with his rage and resentment toward his family of origin for the pain he had endured there. For the first time, he acknowledged he was sexually abused once as a child by a neighbor. Paul struggled (and still does) with telling the truth and being open and honest with me. Emotionally and verbally, he took his anger and pain out on me.

I, on the other hand, did my best to "fix" my husband by letting him know what he needed to do to be all better. In the early days, I thought he was the one with the problem, so he needed to be fixed. I begged, pleaded, sobbed, manipulated, asked too many questions; in short, I tried to control and manage my husband's recovery.

Our communication was miserable; we did not know how to handle conflict in a healthy way that didn't end with Paul raging and me sobbing to the point of throwing up in the bathroom. We fought, slammed doors, gave each other the silent treatment, used each other, shamed each other, said cutting words, many times just trying to keep our heads above the waters of hopelessness.

A turning point came for me in the spring/summer of 2014. After Paul violated his probation, I began to be afraid of staying in our marriage. I desperately needed wise counsel from the perspective of what I loved most: my Catholic Faith. A friend recommended a priest with whom to talk. The first time we met it truly felt like I was sitting at the feet of Jesus. I never felt so validated and understood. I spilled everything. I cried and told him how scared I was and how part of me wanted to leave the nightmare behind.

Father asked me if I loved my husband, and through my tears I whimpered yes. He said I might have grounds for an annulment but that he still saw hope for our marriage. His advice: "Be bold, but don't be a fool." Be bold in fighting for my marriage and Paul's love. But don't be a fool—if it ever got to a point where I no longer felt safe in this marriage, God would see my heart and know I had done all I could.

I began to pray with great faith: "Jesus, if you want me to stay, please make that clear. And if you want me to leave, please make that clear. I want only to do your will." I have my good and bad days, but that prayer is always on my heart.

In the months before and after meeting with the priest, I began to notice significant changes within myself. And it wasn't just me; my mom and close family members noticed it, too. I became less focused on Paul's acting out and recovery process and more focused on taking care of myself and clinging to Jesus. I started to see I was allowing my husband's sexual addiction—which really had nothing to do with me—to control me. It was as if his compulsion had taken control of every area of my life to the point where I didn't even know who I was anymore. I had become so obsessed with controlling Paul's addiction that I almost lost the sense of who I was.

So I began to put my recovery tools to use. I still felt immense hurt, but I cried less and found things to be grateful for every day, even the bad ones. I began to disengage when my husband got angry or was hurtful. If he started to lose his temper, I would calmly tell him that if he was unable to speak to me respectfully then I would leave the room or go for a walk. I was able to keep my emotions in control even when I felt like punching Paul in the nose (which, for a girl who once kicked a hole in a door, was a big victory).

Instead of breaking dishes or picture frames, I would journal my "big feelings" and practice deep breathing. I stopped using "you" statements and began to use "I" statements: "Paul, when I heard you say . . . what I think about that is . . . and that makes me feel . . ." I tried to not focus on whether or not Paul had acted out in a given week; that one still needs growth and practice. I began to place boundaries in our relationship to protect myself from my husband's crazy-making addict behavior. I put specific boundaries in place around our sexual relationship to protect myself from feeling used if he had acted out.

Having a love for writing, I began to journal my feelings, and about everything! I began to pray the Serenity Prayer several times a day while breathing deeply, reminding myself the only person I can control is me. Paul has consistently made choices in our marriage that have caused severe trauma, but I cannot control him. I cannot make Paul well; only Paul can do that. Only he can make the choice to live a life surrendered to recovery.

Most of my life I have compared myself to others, feeling I was never good enough. But I have slowly begun to use the pain as a way to build up my own self-worth. When I began to focus on my own healing, I began to love myself. I allowed myself to feel comfortable in my own skin. I began to use positive self-talk and make time each day to affirm myself. It may sound hokey, but when my self-worth was ripped apart in such an intimate way, learning to love myself just the way I am has been an important step.

I also started to take care of myself physically. I started running by using the "Couch to 5K" program, and I love it! I have already run 5K and 10K races and am planning to run a half-marathon on my next birthday. Running has been a wonderful self-care tool because it's not only good for my body, it's a great way to let out difficult emotions.

I started taking time every day to do at least one thing to nurture my spirit and make me feel good about myself. It could be anything from reading a book to blogging, baking, or painting my nails. In doing so, I started to unlearn some of the lies I had swallowed about this disease. I used to wonder what was so wrong with me that my husband had to go have an affair with himself or look at pornography. I hated myself, thinking somehow I was not pretty or thin enough for Paul so he had to fulfill his needs in an unhealthy, twisted way. I took his sexual addiction personally, carrying the shame and guilt for something that was not even my problem.

But I began to realize that these are *his* problems—they have nothing whatsoever to do with me. These problems plagued Paul long before I came into the picture. He has struggled since he was a young boy, and if he chooses to not surrender himself to recovery, he will only continue on this path of destruction. Acknowledging that was freeing for me, and it helped me grow in my own self-worth and confidence.

I began to read more recovery materials and books, which helped me understand the nature of sex addiction, but more importantly helped dispel lies about myself I had taken on as a result of dealing with this in our marriage. I began another therapy group with my therapist where we went through a recovery workbook for spouses married to a sex addict.

After that summer, Paul became more engaged in recovery. He began to attend several Sexaholics Anonymous groups. He found a sponsor with long-term sobriety and began to work the twelve steps. He is starting to accept that this is something he will have to work at every day of his life. He is beginning to see recovery as a lifestyle instead of a finish line at which he will someday arrive.

Yet it is a slow, painful process to watch. Some days are easier than others. And some days I just want to throw in the towel. Paul has been so out of touch with his feelings for such a long time that he is often unable to be present emotionally for me. I struggle with loneliness, but that only draws me closer to the heart of Jesus, who knew rejection and loneliness in this life.

In working our individual recoveries, we have begun to heal and work at recovery for our marriage, but that is a slow process as well. We found a Recovering Couples Anonymous group in the area, and it has been helpful to work the twelve steps together. We're building emotional intimacy and rekindling love by dating each other again, especially when for my own protection I have put boundaries around physical intimacy. We end our days praying together in bed, sharing two affirmations about the other, and sharing our feelings.

This story is not finished, for I am again at a crossroads in our relationship. In the fall of 2014, I had fresh evidence of Paul's struggle to be honest with me. We had begun to have weekly check-ins to talk about our recovery programs and to discern the state of his sobriety. It was re-traumatizing to find he had again lied about it. We are in the process of working with our therapists to do an official disclosure together. We are considering going out of town to do an intensive three to five days of therapy with a specialist.

I am wrestling with the reality that I am married to a man who, emotionally, is eleven or twelve years old. I am trying to understand what our marriage can look like if my husband is unable to be honest with me. If there is not trust in marriage, how can there be any true intimacy? It's daunting to look into the future, because I truly do not know where we will be. Right now I am taking things one day at a time.

I desperately want our marriage not only to survive all of this, but to thrive. I still have dreams of raising a family together. But the only part I control in the outcome of our story is my piece. I am getting tired, though; we have been married almost three years and my entire experience of my husband has been one of his addiction and lies. At what point do I look at myself in the mirror and acknowledge, honestly, that I can do nothing more? At what point do I say this marriage is beyond repair? Even writing that makes me cry, because leaving my husband is the last thing I want to do.

So right now I take it day by day. I constantly talk to Jesus—in the car going to work, in my head waiting at the bank, while I'm showering, etc. I want to do God's will, and I truly believe God can bring great good out of great evil and pain. I constantly ask Jesus to use all of this for his glory and for our sanctification. This experience has increased my desire to surrender to the will of God and trust his plan, even when the difficulties seem insurmountable.

Initially, I would have never thought there would be so many lessons for me to learn and so many opportunities to grow. I am much more able to trust myself and my gut reaction. I have become much more self-confident; I have learned how to love and accept myself just the way I am. I have realized the only person I can control and change is me.

I idolized my husband when we got married, putting him on a pedestal. And when he fell off that pedestal, boy, did he come crashing down. I had always thought finding the right man would complete my life, perhaps even make me feel better about myself as a person. I realize now it is dangerous to give power like that to another person. Looking for self-fulfillment in a relationship with another human will only disappoint you. The only relationship that will never hurt or disappoint you is the one you have with Jesus.

I cannot say I am grateful my husband is a sex addict; however, I am amazed at and grateful for all the lessons God is teaching me through that addiction that contribute to my own healing and growth.

Unlike a Disney movie, this story's ending is unclear. I cannot look ahead even two or three years. I pray that, whatever the future holds, I will be able to respond in freedom and follow God's will for my life. I find such comfort in the words from the prophet Jeremiah: "For I know the plans I have for you, says the Lord, plans for welfare and not for evil, to give you a future and a hope" (Jer. 29:11). I will never understand why I was dealt this deck of cards; but the more I heal and grow, the more I see God's hand at work. He is using the pain for a purpose; of this I have the utmost confidence.

Stories such as ours, of the trauma caused by sexual addiction, need to be told. The Catholic Church needs to better address this issue; too many lives have been damaged by this disease. I beg priests and deacons to address this issue—there are too many people in the pews suffering in silence. Mine is only one story, but I pray that through it you may find hope and healing.

Beauty Will Rise

By AMY

There is a story in the fifth chapter of the Gospel of Mark that I think the wives of porn addicts should meditate on. It's the story of the woman who had been hemorrhaging for twelve years and thought if she could just touch the hem of Christ's garment, she would be healed. This woman, like many wives of porn addicts, had almost lost hope of ever finding healing. Secondly, she, like many wives, felt her problem was not worth Christ's attention. In spite of this, The Lord Jesus turns toward her. He sees her, he has compassion on her, and he heals her. The wounds are real. They need to be validated and addressed. They are not insignificant. This is something that Amy, whose story you're about to read, learned by the grace of God. She found strength and joy in the presence of her loving savior.

—MATT

If then you have been raised with Christ, seek the things that are above, where Christ is, seated at the right hand of God. Set your minds on things that are above, not on things that are on earth. For you have died, and your life is hid with Christ in God. When Christ who is our life appears, then you also will appear with him in glory (Col. 3:1-4).

Pregnant with my eighth child, I sat in the adoration chapel and cried. I begged Jesus to tell me what was wrong in my marriage. I had spent the past six years fasting and sacrificing for a purpose I didn't understand. I had twisted and conformed and tried to become who I thought my husband wanted me to be. I had worn out the pages of every marriage book that I could get my hands on.

But this day I felt hopeless and alone. Nothing was working. At a recent marriage enrichment seminar, my husband, Jesse, had rated me a zero on almost every aspect of our marriage. That was when I heard the Lord say, "I will reveal all you need to know when you are ready to know it." I sobbed but vowed to be obedient. I had strayed enough in my lifetime and refused to leave his leadership again. I walked out, cried some more, and life carried on.

Fourteen years earlier I had met Jesse, and soon after we were married. I was a single mother with a three-year-old son at the time. My life hadn't been one I was proud of, but I was determined to make a good home for my son.

In those days there was no Internet. There was cable television, though, and video stores galore. I didn't really know what pornography was except for *Playboy* magazine, but I soon learned of the horrors that pornography could bring. Even before our marriage I was aware that Jesse watched these movies on television and was even with him while he rented them at the video store.

I'm not sure what I was thinking beyond what I had learned on *Oprah*—that it was normal, and all guys did it, and if I tried to stop him he would get a real girlfriend. I figured it was better that I knew than he did it in secret. I loathed secrets and lies. So I accepted it, because besides that one "little" indiscretion, he was exactly who I had always hoped to be married to. I turned a blind eye and hoped as we matured he would stop.

But the years passed, and he didn't stop. Sometimes he would talk me into watching with him, but mostly I would walk away. I remember having severe morning sickness and calling for him from the bathroom, but he said his movie was "almost over" and left me there alone. I think that was the first time that I realized this was more than just an adolescent "all guys do it" habit. But I felt powerless to change things. I didn't have a close relationship with God, and the few times I brought it up to my friends, they shrugged their shoulders.

A couple of babies later, and life was pretty fast-paced. We had four young children, and I had begun homeschooling. That's when we got Internet access in our home. Jesse worked in information technology and was much more computer-savvy than I was—not to mention I was naïve. I knew something in our relationship wasn't right, but I couldn't figure out what.

One night, I was out with a friend and confided in her that Jesse often rejected me sexually. I was still young (25) and kept myself in good shape. Still, I knew that I could be cutting with my words and not always as giving as I should be. I vowed that night to be a better wife. I went home excited to tell Jesse of my new resolve.

When I sat down at the computer to check my e-mail before bed, I noticed thumbnail images of naked women down the side bar. I clicked on one and was shocked at what I saw. I had never, even in the movies, seen such things. I asked him if he had put these things on my computer. He said he was "just curious" and wouldn't do it again. I don't know what it was about the computer images that somehow seemed more pervasive than the movies, but it shook me to my core. I demanded that he stop all of it—movies, Internet, everything. He said he would never do it again.

Finally, I sought God in all of this. I didn't know how to pray, but I tried. I surrounded myself with friends who seemed to understand morality in a way that I never had, and I was inspired to search for that morality in my own life. In the meantime, I became pregnant with our fifth child. I thought things were going better, although there was still that part of me that was unsure.

A few months after our fifth child was born, I was showing a friend something on my computer and the cookies popped up. There were hundreds of pornographic websites. I could track back for more than a year. This time, I wasn't just stunned, I was furious. He had given his word, and he had lied. Still young and naïve, I once again took him at his word. I knew nothing of sex addiction or how pornography can be just as addictive as drugs.

We got marriage counseling, but for some reason I never brought up this issue. I was ashamed and embarrassed. I believed him when he said he had stopped. I desperately wanted our marriage to work. I started fasting and taking cold showers and praying frequently for Jesse and our marriage. My life changed radically in a way only God can make happen. I thought Jesse's did, too. When we spoke of pornography and inappropriate movies, we seemed to be on the same page. He began attending Catholic men's conferences and praying with us as a family.

Babies six and seven came along. We visited the beach every year with my family, and I was always self-conscious among the hundreds of women in bikinis. I asked Jesse if he was looking at them, and he always said no and that I was beautiful. I didn't really believe him, but I buried my anxieties. If I did bring them up, he got defensive and accused me of being untrusting, crazy, "insane." I had low self-esteem, so I took him at his word and tried harder to be the wife he needed.

Then there was that day in adoration. That day kept me coming back to God. Waiting, watching, listening. For years, I thought my inability to forgive Jesse was ruining our marriage and family. We were tight on funds, so I didn't feel right seeking counseling.

While pregnant with baby number ten, I became determined to figure this thing out once and for all. By then pornography addiction was finally being talked about, so there were some books on healing as the spouse of an addict. I didn't think Jesse was an addict, but I shared a lot of the pain and feelings that the spouses in the books did. I read books on men who had been addicts but had recovered. I read books on the science of pornography addiction. I read Christian and non-Christian books alike. I confessed my lack of forgiveness at least thirty times in the sacrament of reconciliation.

Finally, I found a Catholic therapist who agreed to see me for free. When I met with him, I described my failings and weaknesses. I was searching for help with my seeming inability to forgive Jesse for his past—what I called—"indiscretions." The therapist asked me to describe my husband. I talked about how Jesse had always been a hands-on dad, active in our church and community, always the guy that helped others move or with childcare. He had always willingly changed diapers and let me go out with friends. He attended Catholic men's retreats and groups, listened to Christian music, and read Christian publications. Everything on the outside seemed like I was married to a strong man of God.

Within fifteen minutes of my description, the therapist told me that Jesse had been lying to me for years and that my "hunches" may have been God telling me that my husband was an addict. He explained how sex addicts have the ability to live two very different lives. The "good" that they do is almost always an over-the-top goodness to compensate for the secret lives they are living.

I couldn't believe it. Our eleventh baby was just nine weeks old. In the two years before that, we had attended and even been speakers at several marriage retreats. Things seemed better, except that I couldn't forget the past. The counselor asked me to do a very hard thing: ask Jesse if he was being truthful. I was afraid to ask, afraid of his response, and mostly I didn't want to know the truth.

I waited for a day that felt like a lifetime but finally worked up the courage to ask. His answer blew up my entire world. He hadn't stopped. He had lied all those times and for all those years. He had worked around the Internet security on our computer. He had hidden it all from me.

Those first few weeks after disclosure were brutal. I lost fourteen pounds in ten days. I cried almost nonstop, and I barely slept. I found support at a spouse support group at a nearby parish. Jesse and I were in counseling together. For the first time, I focused purely on getting myself healthy and well. I read, I prayed, I trusted in God alone. I knew only his grace could repair our marriage. I knew with eleven children I had to give every ounce of myself to make a home for them that wasn't broken. Jesus truly carried us in those months after Jesse's first disclosure.

I sensed Jesse wasn't telling me everything. After a while, I approached him about it. This time he did confess everything. And I mean everything. My heart was shattered. Internet pornography was hardly the worst of it.

But God's timing is always perfect, and though I grieved like I didn't know was possible, I also rejoiced, because the truth was finally out. All those years of wondering what was wrong were over. Now we could start anew. Jesse said he was committed to staying clean, and his behavior backed that up. I was committed to learning about what real mercy and forgiveness involved.

In the early stages of recovery, I learned what most spouses of all kinds of addicts learn—to put one hundred percent trust in God and trust only the behavior of the addict. His words are meaningless. I knew that if Jesse's second disclosure was not everything or that if he relapsed and lied to me, God—not Jesse—would tell me what I needed to know. So far God had come through for me, even when my reliance on him was weak. We also learned in recovery that, after God, we can trust ourselves and our instincts. The Holy Spirit will place on our hearts the truth, and we are right to listen to him.

> *Put to death therefore what is earthly in you: fornication, impurity, passion, evil desire, and covetousness, which is idolatry. On account of these the wrath of God is coming. In these you once walked, when you lived in them. But now put them all away: anger, wrath, malice, slander, and foul talk from your mouth. Do not lie to one another, seeing that you have put off the old nature with its practices and have put on the new nature, which is being renewed in knowledge after the image of its creator. Here there cannot be Greek and Jew, circumcised and uncircumcised, barbarian, Scythian, slave, free man, but Christ is all, and in all (Col. 3:5—11).*

This past year has taught me a lot of things, but probably the biggest one is that this addiction is not something our spouses do to us. One of the first things I learned in recovery was that we almost always marry our emotional equals. When Jesse and I married, I was twenty-one and he was twenty-two, but emotionally I was probably around seventeen. He was similar in his emotional age. As the marriage goes on, the person with the addiction doesn't mature. He remains at the age he was emotionally when the addiction began. The spouse moves forward, and the gap between them continues to widen.

I have learned in recovery that addicts manipulate to protect their secret. When everything started coming to light, I
felt as though I had been living in an alternate universe for all
those years. At one point, I was prescribed an antidepressant.
I didn't really feel depressed, but I did feel anxious all of the
time, and I would fly off the handle at the slightest thing.

While I was on the medication, my instincts were stunted
even more, and his addiction was at its worst. In recovery, I
have heard other women describe the medications that they
were put on to control their "crazy" suspicions. Of course,
there is nothing wrong with medication when it's necessary,
but I have found it is over-prescribed for too many women
in my situation.

It has been nearly a year since Jesse's first disclosure. We just
welcomed our twelfth baby. I believe there has been significant healing on both sides and within our marriage. I know
we have a long way to go. Those first months after disclosure,
I spent a lot of time questioning God, my faith, my instincts. I
wanted out of this whole mess. I wanted it over.

A friend reminded me that the only way out of it is to go
through it. I went through and continue to go through the
stages of grief. One day I feel fantastic, and another day I feel
like it all happened yesterday. I have been forced to admit my
faults and focus not on what he did but on who I want to be. I
have learned that forgiveness is not the same as trust. I forgive
Jesse. I do not fully trust him, but I hope one day I will.

I often wonder what the fallout of this addiction has done,
or will do, to our children. Our oldest child is aware of Jesse's addiction. He is twenty years old and married. He has
a forgiving and understanding heart and has acted accord-
ingly. Our next oldest is eighteen and was obviously aware
that something was going on. She knew about my counseling
appointments and our support groups. On the advice of a

therapist, Jesse told her that he had lied to me and hurt our marriage and that we were working to restore it.

The rest of the children haven't been told anything, but I believe honesty is the best policy, so at some point they will be. Details are not necessary, of course, but a general outline is recommended. Our children have been raised to know Jesus, to understand mercy, and embrace forgiveness. I trust that when the time is right and they know the truth, they will react in a loving way.

When this all began, I said again and again, "I want what God wants." Since Jesse has chosen recovery, right now it feels safe to remain in the marriage. I believe what God wants is for Jesse to be healthy and to remain in the light. I believe that God wants our marriage to heal. I know that Satan does not want those things. As I have learned to grieve and set boundaries, I've also asked Jesus again and again to let me be able to see Jesse as he does. I have been reminded to work on my sins and weaknesses, because that's all I can control.

Once I made the choice to remain in the marriage, I learned that at some point you have to end marriage number one and begin again with marriage number two. We are working toward doing that. Old habits and beliefs creep back in sometimes.

I wish none of this had ever happened, but it did, so I choose to be grateful for all of it. I never thought I would say that, but I truly feel it in my heart. I have been lifted out of a pit by the hand of God and shown that I am nothing without God but I really can "do all things through Christ who gives me strength" (Phil. 4:13).

I have the utmost respect for the men and women who fight this addiction. In the spouses of addicts I see a strength that I never knew existed. I have learned empathy and sympathy, and I have let go of so many things I once viewed as important. Because of this experience, I was able to do things I once thought impossible, like finishing my bachelor's degree after seventeen years of being out of school. Truly, when we give God the reins, amazing things can happen.

"Tears in the night but joy comes in the morning" (Psalm 30:5).

As of this writing, even though we are still in the first year of recovery, I have seen significant changes in Jesse, our marriage, and myself. I am grateful for all of the books, articles, websites, certified sex addiction counselors, and support groups. Even five years ago such resources were few and far between. Even in my darkest days, when it was hard to feel hope, I knew hope was there.

I believe if there are two willing participants that relationships can be saved. It takes dedication and hard work—and copious amounts of prayer and sacrifice—but they can be saved. I have seen others who have spouses who haven't chosen recovery seek recovery on their own and go on to have healthy lives either alone or with a new spouse.

A couple of days after Jesse's first disclosure, I was reading the story of St. Faustina to the children during our morning devotion time. The last paragraph read, "Jesus told St. Maria Faustina, 'I expect you to show mercy always and everywhere. You cannot excuse yourself from this.' The best way to show that we trust in the mercy of Jesus is to be merciful and forgiving to the people who hurt us. Are we willing to do this?" I wept as I read it, because I knew what Jesus was asking me to do, and I knew I could not do it alone.

I pray all of you will find peace and recovery in your situations. Restoration is possible. I've seen it, and I've lived it.

Released and Restored

By ANA

*Some things can only be healed by the antiseptic light of truth.
One of those things is pornography addiction. Pornography
breaks a man's inner world into fragments. He is no longer
integrated. There are parts of him, parts of his heart, that the
shame that comes through sexual sin has taught him to keep
hidden. And so, to one degree or another, he lives a lie. He acts
one way with his wife, he acts an entirely different way in the
den late at night while his family is asleep. Ana shares how even
several years into her marriage she was completely clueless to her
husband's porn addiction. While his eventual admission to
having used porn felt nothing less than if he had confessed
adultery, that moment was the moment healing began.*
                                                    —MATT

"You may as well have told me that you've been having an
affair our entire marriage."

Those were the words that I tearfully uttered to my husband, Ryan, on a cold evening in February. That was the day
he revealed to me that he had an addiction to pornography,
an addiction that began in middle school and from which he
was just then finding freedom.

My husband and I had a fairly quick courtship and engagement. In a little less than six years of marriage we had weathered several relocations for his employment and three miscarriages and been blessed with two beautiful children, with a third on the way. Generally we were happy, and our marriage appeared to be intact.

Both of us knew, however, that there was something brewing under the surface. I was unaware of what it was, but it was slowly pulling us apart. I kept telling myself that this was just the season of life we were in—*We're busy, we have two young children, and we're both working; we'll get through this.*

That night in February, while driving, I was listening to a Christian call-in radio program. A caller described how her husband was addicted to pornography and she was seeking advice. I listened out of curiosity and pity. *How could you be married to someone for over twenty years and not know that he was addicted to pornography? That poor woman. She must not be giving her husband something that he needs, so he was forced to look elsewhere.*

As those thoughts ran through my mind, I heard a little voice speak to me. It's the voice that puts an idea in your head and sometimes gives you a bad feeling in the pit of your stomach, because you know you are going to have to choose to act on it or else ignore it. It was the voice, I believe, of God: "You need to ask your husband if he struggles with pornography."

Upon arriving home, I knew I had to ask my husband about this, even though it was going to be uncomfortable and—at least to him—coming out of nowhere. We put our children to bed and, from what I remember, I confronted Ryan bluntly: "Do you ever look at porn?" I felt sheepish and just wanted the conversation to be over as soon as he told me no.

However, as I looked at his face, I saw surprise, humility, shame, and sadness. "Ana," he said, "I've wanted to talk to you ..."

At that moment, it was as if my hearing became muffled. I could suddenly hear my heartbeat in my ears, and my breathing seemed to be louder than the words my husband was saying. I took a deep breath, and we sat down on the couch. My husband confessed to me that he had been addicted to pornography since he was a teenager.

My mind was racing.

I felt angry, ashamed, sad, frustrated, and hurt. I was trying to make sense of my own thoughts and emotions. I felt a lump in my throat growing larger until it caused tears to stream from my eyes as I asked him, "We have been married for almost six years. When is the last time you looked at it?" I wanted him to tell me that this pornography problem was over before we were married, but in my heart, I knew that wasn't the case.

"It's been about six months since I've looked at anything," he said.

The anger and the hurt were too much for me to handle. All I could say was, "You may as well have told me that you have been having an affair our entire marriage."

We sat in awkward silence as I gathered my thoughts and he awaited my reaction. So many questions were racing through my mind, but I wasn't sure I wanted to know the answers: *When was this happening? Can I ever leave him alone with the computer again? He hid this from me for over six years, what else could he be hiding from me? We have a daughter, doesn't he know that the women he was looking at are someone else's daughters? What does he get from those images that I'm not giving him?* I knew this was not a discussion that we would resolve that evening. I knew that it was going to take a lot of work to rebuild our relationship—a lot of work for which, honestly, I didn't know if I was ready.

At that moment, I was a working mother of two young children, in my first trimester with our third child. I was tired. And now I was emotionally exhausted and felt as though I had just become disconnected from the only person I trusted with my true self, my whole heart.

I felt completely alone, and that loneliness made me numb and apathetic. The walls of my heart were up and heavily guarded, and I wasn't sure I would allow my husband—or anyone, for that matter—to break through them ever again. I remember thinking that maybe I should just blow this off and deescalate the entire situation by pretending that I had known all along and wasn't as hurt as I was. That "solution" appeared to be a whole lot easier than the work that would surely be ahead of us.

But while sitting silent on the couch across from my husband, my eyes kept finding the large crucifix that adorned our living room wall. My thoughts began drifting toward Christ. Looking at his pierced hands and feet, I knew he knew what it was to suffer. He—if no one else—knew the pain I felt.

For the first time in my life, I felt a desperate need to invite God into my heart. This was going to require a lot work, since I had not nurtured my relationship with God beyond attending weekly Mass. It was going to require honesty so that I could truly let God in. I wasn't sure I was ready for it. It seemed that my burden suddenly had become even bigger—I had to fix my marriage *and* fix my relationship with God.

Being apathetic would likely hurt me more in the long run, and trying to resolve all of this alone seemed impossible. By the grace of God, I came to realize that my burden is light with his help. This hurt was so deep in my heart, it could be healed only with his help. After all of this came to light, I didn't feel alone anymore. The eyes of my soul were open to see that God was with me, and he had been with me all of this time.

Feeling God's presence seemed to happen in a divine, fleeting moment. I was still hurt, crying, sitting there on the couch with my husband who was just as upset. I told him that I planned to contact our parish priest to see what my options were for beginning some sort of healing, whether it was counseling or someone with whom to talk.

There were a few big-ticket items I needed to ask my husband about right then and there. I needed to know that he had remained physically faithful to me, which he confirmed he had. I also needed to know that he had told his sins to a priest in confession, and he had. The last thing I needed to know was what he planned to do to make sure this wouldn't happen again.

It became apparent to me that my husband had, in fact, taken these actions seriously, and he surprised me as he laid out some practical interventions. He had installed internet monitoring software on his computer, and he also discussed his plans for establishing not one but several accountability partners, friends he could contact and pray with at a moment's notice, should he feel tempted to view pornography. Feeling somewhat satisfied for the moment, this was all that my heart and my mind could handle for one evening.

We went to bed that night and, despite my exhaustion, I could hardly sleep. It felt as though my blood was boiling. Lying there in the darkness, the anger and hurt consumed me and I was beginning to pity myself. *How could he do this to me? What did I do to deserve this? How could I be so foolish to think he actually loved me? No one can know about this.*

As that latter thought crossed my mind, God's grace showed me that I had my own shame with which to deal. My husband had verbalized his experience of the immense shame that came with such an addiction. This shame that he carried was the biggest factor holding him back from confessing to me and from seeking help and healing sooner. But why would I have shame to deal with? Wasn't this his problem, and wasn't I just the victim?

While lying there, analyzing my own feelings, I imagined discussing this situation with my friends and family. I cringed thinking about their reactions. In my imagination, they would surely think that our marriage had no merit. They would certainly think that my husband was a pervert. They would pity me for being stuck in an unhappy marriage.

I had made an effort to project a happy, satisfying marriage to our friends and families. My husband and I didn't ever argue in front of others outside of little quips here and there, so how was I supposed to reveal that not only were we suddenly having a hard time, I was oblivious to something that my husband had been doing our entire relationship?

The shame that engrossed me had to be overcome if I was going to start healing, because I needed to talk to people about this. I needed to talk to people who truly cared for my husband and me and who would pray for our relationship. That night I fell asleep silently crying out to God to rid me of my own shame, and inviting him into my suffering so that my spouse and I could begin to heal.

The next few days were difficult. My husband and I were not talking much to each other; he thought I needed space to comprehend and process the situation. For my part, I couldn't look at him without wanting to slap him or run away crying—yet a part of me wanted to just fall into his loving embrace.

I reached out to our parish priest via e-mail because I could not talk about things without bursting into tears. The next day I received a response from him that was immensely helpful. He stated, "The resolution of this in your heart and relationship depends on a few factors: 1) your ability and willingness to forgive your husband, 2) your ability to acknowledge the hurt it has done to you and to identify where the pain really is so as to prevent you from jumping to false conclusions, and 3) your willingness to ask Jesus to come into the pain and wound it caused to bring his light and healing to both of your hearts and your relationship."

Meditating on each of those suggestions helped me focus on the steps I needed to take. I had already offered prayers asking Jesus to join me in my suffering. This brought me an indescribable consolation, because until I was able to conquer my own shame, I did not feel that I could talk to anyone about this, which made me feel very lonely. Praying daily to Jesus and Mary and asking them to come with me into this pain, asking them to hold me and join me in my suffering, was sometimes the only thing that would get me out of bed and on my feet.

One by one, I thought through the priest's suggestions. Was I willing and able to forgive my husband? With God's grace, absolutely. Even as Ryan confessed to me, through my hurt and anger, the thought never crossed my mind that this was the end for us. In my storm of emotions that night as he told me about his pornography addiction, I never stopped loving him or caring about him or his soul. We made a promise to God—a promise to work unceasingly on getting each other to heaven. We had built a family together, and this entire problem was something that, with God's grace, we were going to not only survive but come out of with a stronger and healthier marriage.

As certain as I was that I was able to forgive my husband, I had to come to understand and realize that this was not going to happen right then and there. Forgiveness was going to have to entail the choice to continue to love my husband and show him so, in the midst of a broken heart. But this is difficult, and that is where I learned to lean on God. Some days, even months after the initial confession, anger would swell up in me, and I would be just as infuriated with my husband as I was the night everything came to light.

However, with God's grace, I was able to rise above the anger and still, genuinely, love my husband. Forgiveness also meant I was going to have to be honest with my husband, more honest than I had ever been before, so that he could understand how everything had affected me and how I was feeling. This meant I could no longer respond to him in a monotone, "I'm fine," when I was really hurting inside. I needed to ask God consistently to help me assess my feelings and then be able to turn the revelations into words and relay them to my husband.

As I mentioned before, it seemed easier to just lie and say that I was fine when I was not. Then I could ignore my feelings. By ignoring my feelings, I was able to forget about them all together until the next time I was hurt or upset—then the unspoken feelings would swell up tenfold, which would lead to pain, broken communication, and a broken relationship.

Continuing to follow my parish priest's advice, I had to ask God to show me the very roots of my hurt. Through my daily, meditative prayer, God pointed out the areas where I was most hurt. For the first time in my life, I felt as though I was being honest with God, and with myself. I've always been aware that I am not a woman with high self-esteem. I use humor to distract people from my slightly overweight physique and my character flaws.

As Ryan told me about how he turned to porn when we were having difficulties, I couldn't help but think that I was actually pushing him toward porn. I remember the deluded thoughts that came pouring into my mind: *"It's because I'm not as pretty and skinny as the porn stars. It's because I don't satisfy him sexually."* Instead of realizing Ryan had an addiction, I assumed it was my flaws that drove him to the pornography. I believed it was all my fault.

I laid down this burden before the Lord in prayer, and thankfully, with the grace of God, I was enlightened to the fact that Ryan's pornography addiction did not have to do with my physique, and it did not have to do with me not satisfying him sexually. It did not have to do with anything that I did or didn't do, or how I looked, or how I acted. God gently told me that this wasn't about me. This was my husband's cross to bear. I could either keep my heart hardened toward Ryan, making his faith journey more difficult, or I could continue to seek God's graces to soften my heart and, like Simon helped Jesus, I could help Ryan carry his cross and lead him closer to Jesus.

Still, there were questions whose answers I wasn't finding in prayer. One of them stuck in my mind: why couldn't Ryan realize that each woman that he lusted after was someone's daughter? At the time, we had a daughter of our own and were expecting our second daughter in the fall. He would not want someone lusting after our daughters, so why was he being such a hypocrite? We also have a son together; surely, he would never want our son lusting after women. When our children were born, why didn't he think of all of this and just stop looking at porn?

I took these questions to a friend who had walked a similar journey with her husband. They also have two young daughters, and I wanted to see how she would answer my questions. Her response was eye-opening. She said that pornography was an addiction her husband was fighting—"like those who smoke or drink too much. It was something that he struggled with and he worked hard to overcome."

Hearing her compare pornography to substance abuse, for the first time I pondered the idea of pornography being an actual addiction. This was something that he did not want to do but could not stop himself. His brain and body had become dependent on those images. I remembered Ryan telling me that certain images could trigger sexual desire in him; things I had never considered because they don't affect me like they affect him. Certain images in music videos, commercials, and magazines with women in underwear; movies with sex scenes; at any moment these images could produce a desire in him to look at more.

This epiphany changed things in our daily lives. I had to call and ask to be removed from a popular lingerie company's catalogue subscription list, and we had to research and review movies before sitting down and watching them. Ultimately, these changes were better for the both of us, and it is refreshing to be able to openly talk to my husband about his triggers. I do not miss the catalogue, and we have been able to enjoy some wholesome movies that we may not have otherwise watched.

While my friend helped me understand that one can truly be addicted to pornography, my concern about my husband's lack of empathy toward the subjects being someone's children still bothered me. To this, my friend went on to say about her husband's porn addiction, "I knew that having little girls, it had to have eaten at him. I knew he was not proud, he was downright disgusted with himself."

Ryan had said those exact words to me: "I don't want to look at it, then I do, and I'm disgusted with myself." This is where things really started to come full circle for me. Of course he was not able to simply stop looking at porn like I thought he should be able to—he had a true addiction! He was not spineless because he couldn't realize that these were daughters. He knew that, but he was addicted—he couldn't talk himself out of his physical and mental desire for more.

All of this brought an unexpected peace to my heart. It helped me realize that being addicted to porn did not define my husband. He was still the same strong, loving, kind, generous, and empathetic man I fell in love with.

As with anyone who struggles with addiction, the road to recovery is not smooth. Several months after Ryan's initial confession, I found myself reviewing a Covenant Eyes report that flagged numerous "mature content" sites. As I was reading through the log, I was relieved to see that they were all websites I had gone to when looking for some help with breastfeeding issues with our newest daughter.

I was just finishing up glancing at the report when suddenly a date and time in the mature content report caught my eye. I looked closer; the site had been accessed when I knew I had been away from home. I looked closer and saw that there was only one link, one click, and then the computer activity ceased. My heart sank. This could not be happening. I thought we were over this. The feelings that I felt that night in February rushed back to me.

Thanks to the process of healing I had gone through, my heart and mind immediately turned to prayer: *"Lord, please come with me into this hurt. Hold my hand. No, not just my hand, hold me. Hug me. Let me feel your embrace and your love as I hurt. Holy Spirit, please come. Be with me. Guide my thoughts and my words. Help me find the words to say to confront my husband in a loving manner so as to help him continue to sin no more."*

I confronted my husband, and he told me that he was tempted. In fact, he explained to me that he will always be tempted on a daily basis, and it is only through God's help and grace that he does not succumb to the temptation more often. In this particular instance, he had been feeling spiritually attacked—the world was weighing on him and he was tempted to go to that "fix" that made him feel better temporarily. Coincidentally, our prayer life together had been attacked as well, and we were rarely praying together on a daily basis.

It was obvious this temptation Ryan faced, and began acting on, was different. He said that after he clicked to a link that contained mature content, he immediately stopped himself from going any further, shut the computer, and texted a group of his accountability partners, who prayed for him immediately. I could see the hurt in his eyes as he was telling me this. I knew he was being truthful, but he was ashamed for even letting the temptation take him that far.

It really hit home: this is not an addiction that my husband will get over and that will never again rear its ugly head— he will be tempted with this for the rest of his life, which means it is going to be around for the rest of *our* lives together. The process of hurt, forgiveness, and healing that I had gone through may have to happen again. But as long as my relationship with the Lord is intact, I will be able to remain hopeful, love my husband completely, continue to forgive him, and help him carry his cross as he works toward his eternal reward.

Nearly a year after that night in February, I am amazed at how one confession could take me on such a journey of faith. I never could have imagined how much emotional and spiritual work I would have to put forth in order for God to restore my emotional health and my marriage. For several weeks after learning of my husband's porn addiction, he and I committed to a period of sexual abstinence, which helped me heal further emotionally. This period of abstinence restored and reset our deep desire and love for each other in a whole new way.

Ryan and I also make a continual effort to further develop and nourish our prayer life together. This is something we have worked on our entire marriage. Having that daily prayer time with my husband is a direct and beautiful way to invite God into our marriage, and a new way to communicate to each other.

Since that fateful night when my eyes were opened to a side of my husband I never knew existed, I can say that, thanks be to God, my heart is healing, and I have forgiven Ryan and will continue to forgive him if need be. All the glory for overcoming this goes to God for wrapping me in his loving embrace and carrying me through this suffering, all while placing the right people in my path who would offer words of encouragement and healing. Although our lives and marriage are still a far cry from perfect, and Ryan still faces temptation on a daily basis, this entire journey has drawn us closer to God—and for that, I will be forever thankful.

Learning to Love My Dad

By MAYA

Every daughter longs to be seen by her Daddy. My daughters are like that. I'll hear my wife say to them, after getting them dressed, "Go show Daddy how pretty you look," and then, the eager patter of tiny feet, and, "Daddy! Look at me!" When a daughter asks this of her father, she's really asking, "Who am I?" "Do you notice me?" "Am I lovely?" This dependence upon one's father for identity naturally lessens throughout our lives, but never goes away completely. How heartbreaking, how piercingly disappointing, to discover that "Daddy" looks at porn. I once heard of a teenage girl who said, after she discovered her father's porn use, "I used to look up to him, now I can't even look at him." But Jesus calls us to love our parents. In this case, it will require Maya to walk the middle path between blaming everything on her father and justifying his behavior with, "This is just something all guys do, I guess." Maya shares how she walked this middle path and how you can too.

—MATT

As time passes, our lives become a collection of memories. Some are joyful, and some are painful to the point you wish you could forget them. Until I was sixteen years old, I didn't have any memories I wished I could forget. My life was seemingly normal for any girl in a practicing Catholic family—preparing for my senior year in high school, spending time with friends, going on innocent adventures, and deepening my faith. My life wasn't perfect; it simply went on like a calm dream. Then, on a cold night, a moment of terrible realization thrust me into a nightmare.

I learned that my father was a longtime porn addict.

It came as a shock. I instantly felt a dark, sinking feeling, and my eyes swelled with hot tears as I grasped an old rosary for comfort. My father never abused me, nor did I ever find any trace of pornography anywhere. That made the shock even worse, because it was the last thing I expected. All it took was finding my mother weeping, and a not-so-lucky guess as I tried to comfort her. They had kept the secret for years—but now it was out, and I didn't know how to process it.

From studying the Theology of the Body, I was aware of the destructive nature of pornography, yet I never suspected it was lurking in my own home or that my dad was a slave to it. Because I was young and discovering my own unique identity as a female and daughter of God, I deeply cherished the virtues of modesty and chastity.

I assumed my father wasn't touched by the poison of pornography, since it's the opposite of those virtues. I always thought he was better than that. I saw him as immune to it, even unbreakable. Little did I know that the poison had been in effect for years. After my blindfold was torn off, bits and pieces from my childhood and current teen years began to make sense in a way they hadn't before. It was like I was hit by a heavy wave of raw realization for which I wasn't prepared. It's difficult to face that a loved one is a porn addict, because it comes like a knife in the dark.

Despite an average childhood, I grew up with a quiet

wound in my heart. I always felt distant and detached from my dad, emotionally and physically. I often felt awkward, ugly, and insecure, because he rarely affirmed or embraced me. This left a bitter pang of emptiness that I could never put into words. Though I do have happy memories with my dad, I grew up lacking the male affirmation all girls need from their father.

Every little girl wants to feel loved and regarded as a princess by the first man in her life—her daddy. The porn industry stole that from me. Pornography builds a façade between the user and itself. While it may seem that it remains hidden and doesn't affect anyone, the reality is that it alienates the user from those around him. And, for daughters, that alienation can be devastating. I knew I loved my dad dearly and vice versa, yet we were two strangers living under the same roof; and in my innocence, I could never understand why.

Later I realized: how could I expect him to bond with me when he had conditioned himself to view women as nothing more than objects to be used for pleasure? He couldn't be the father he was supposed to be, because he wasn't being the man God expected him to be. Pornography unravels many of the virtues a true man is intended to possess, virtues so crucial to fatherhood. With all of this dawning on me in the span of one night—the lost relationship with my father and the bitter reality of the situation—my heart was broken.

Soon afterward, my dad tearfully apologized for his actions, and for the first time he told me of his own traumatic past. While it offered insight, the hurt remained. He promised to recover and began right away to make plans to do so. Yet for a long time I could not look at him the same. My large family was on the verge of being broken because of his problem, and I couldn't even think of him as my God-given father.

I became distrusting of men. For some time, I recoiled at

the sight of them. I couldn't help but wonder if they also struggled with—or embraced!—pornography. My father was the one who was supposed to protect me against other men's lustful thoughts, yet he was right there along with them. I thought, if he has fallen to this, how can I ever trust anyone else?

Throughout all of this, my mother was the forgotten victim. It killed me to know that she was suffering more than she let me see. My mother has always been strong, but she became someone I didn't recognize. I wanted to comfort her, and while we would come together to cry and rally ourselves, I knew she was suffering a deep hurt that I could not take away. Though I prayed for her sorrows to be lifted, the knowledge of them only added to the pain and hurt.

A person can handle only so much interior turmoil before she reaches a breaking point. Though I had my mom, I felt that there was no one I could go to. I was so ashamed and embarrassed to speak of a sin so near me. It remained bottled up, and I numbly trudged on. But remaining stagnant only made matters worse—I wasn't allowing myself to heal. However, despite the pain and seeming hopelessness, God was working with my brokenness. He makes all things new, and, slowly, I began to forgive my dad.

The first step was to surrender it all to God, including the broken ugliness of it all. It took many visits to the Blessed Sacrament in adoration, countless prayers, and the magnitude of God's grace and mercy. It was only through his goodness that he was able to heal my broken heart and grant me the grace to forgive.

As I did so, I realized that when I had felt abandoned, fatherless, and unlovable, God was there, pouring out his quiet love on me. When I thought I was alone and unprotected, he was there, sheltering and protecting me. Though I couldn't see it at the time, he had never left me—or my dad. It reminded me of the words of the great sinner turned saint, Augustine: "In my deepest wound I saw your glory, and it dazzled me."

My relationship with my dad gradually repaired, and I grew to love and respect him once more. After many years, the pang of emptiness was silenced for the both of us. I firmly believe that my dad finally saw the monstrosity that pornography is when he realized the damage that had been seeping into his life, though silently, to grave effect. However, he had the courage and humility to face it, root it out of his life, and allow himself to be healed—for the sake of not only himself, but also of his family.

Through this he came to understand what true masculinity is and rose up to be the father and husband God called him to be. Despite my earlier anger with my dad, I never stopped praying for him. Right when it seemed hopeless, God repaired the failing hope. He showed me that there is no amount of brokenness he cannot restore when we allow him. Even in the ugliness of sin, he never ceased to call my dad, and me, back to himself, because he was and is the only one who can satisfy the intrinsic yearning we have for him.

Though the world tries to drown out and fill that desire with toxic counterfeits such as pornography, nothing can or will satisfy us but God alone. Once again, the words of St. Augustine rang true: "You have made us for yourself, oh Lord, and our hearts are restless until they rest in you."

What Can I Do About Me?

By RHYLL

It would be nice, wouldn't it, if there was a six-week program out there, a set of prayers, or a book, at the end of which one could say, "That's it! I'm free of the temptation to look at pornography!" But there isn't. Recovery from porn and sex addiction isn't something that happens to you; it isn't an event. Rather, it's a daily—sometimes hourly—choice through the decisions we make. Many wives of porn addicts can get so focused on their husband's recovery that they forget about their own. And just as there are no quick fixes for porn addicts, there are no quick fixes for the wives who have suffered betrayal trauma at the hands of the one who promised to be faithful "until death do us part." Rhyll describes, very honestly, the pain and bewilderment she experienced over her husband's porn addiction, but also how, over time and through witnessing the determination of her husband to live a life free of sexual sin, she was able to begin trusting and even respecting her husband once more. Rhyll and her husband are a living testimony to the fact that the road to recovery is tough, bloody tough, but that God's grace is tougher.

—MATT

It was a beautiful fall Sunday morning and my family was on its way to church. As we entered the church building, I could sense something was wrong with my husband. But I was focused on responsibilities at church, so I was taken off guard when Steven said, "I need to talk to you." Those words, even today, nine years later, bring fear to my heart, because that wasn't the first time I had heard my husband say them with fear in his eyes. In thirty-two years of marriage, he had disclosed twice before this day his betrayal and double life. So, that Sunday morning I expected the worst.

But it was even worse than I anticipated. My husband told me he had been arrested two weeks earlier for picking up a prostitute. He had kept it a secret, but the shame was eating at him, and he knew he had to come clean in order to live with himself.

That day I had my first major "surrender to God" experience. On our front lawn after church, when he told me of his arrest, I turned my palms upward, looked to heaven, and quietly spoke to God: "Take him, I can't do this anymore." My plea for heavenly help was heard and answered in that moment, because, even with the crisis that was facing us in our marriage and our family, I had a sense of peace that can come only from God.

I thought our marriage was over. I would no longer have my home, and I would need to find a way to provide for my family. This disclosure was different from the first two. Thirteen years into our marriage, my husband disclosed that he had started using pornography as a little boy. His first exposure was at the age of six and he was drawn to the nervous excitement that pornography offered. He actually handed over the first pornographic magazine to his mother, who obviously did not know how to handle the situation and did nothing.

His behavior escalated through high school, and even

though he confessed to his church leader, no one knew how serious the issue was or how to help him. When I was nineteen and Steven was twenty, we met at church. We fell in love and married without him sharing any information about his pornography use and sexual acting out. He thought that our marriage and sexual relationship would solve his need for pornography.

He began traveling as part of his work, and over a period of several years his behavior escalated to frequenting strip clubs and then to hiring prostitutes. The man I knew and loved was a successful businessman, involved in the community and in church and the father of our five children at that time. I was devastated by his disclosure. No one would have guessed that he lived a double life.

When he first disclosed this, he was very emotional and expressed deep regret and shame. I was in shock. I felt naïve to the ways of the world and could not believe that someone to whom I had given my life would behave in such a way. I cried softly as he told me, and I felt isolated in my pain. With whom could I share such shameful information? Who would understand? Even I didn't understand. But with the help of a loving and kind church leader, who encouraged Steven to repent and not look back, and me to forgive and be a "helpmate," we moved forward.

Ten years later, early on a weekday morning, Steven came to me in our bedroom and said those dreaded words: "I need to talk to you." This time he cried bitter tears and said he didn't know why he continued to do such things. While he was able to remain "sober" (no acting-out behavior) for three years, for the past seven years his behavior had escalated back to frequenting strip clubs and prostitutes. He feared that he had contracted a sexually transmitted disease and was afraid I might find out.

I was so angry that I wanted to yell at him, but I didn't want our children to hear. Instead, I said in a piercing whisper, "Why can't you stop doing this? You are throwing away your whole life." Through his tears, he told me it was not my fault and that he wanted to change. In my frustration and outrage, I kept repeating "*Why?*", but he couldn't answer.

At the time of Steven's first disclosure, I focused on trying to forget. The second time was much more confusing, and I tried to assert myself more. Sometimes I loved him and wanted to take care of him, but I still hated what he had done— the infidelity, the lies, the deceit, and the double life. When he came home in the evening, I would see him and feel upset. Even though his presence brought out a toxic reaction in me, I desperately wanted him to love and validate me. We spent hours talking but never came to any conclusions. He felt shame and I felt total frustration.

I wanted to shield our seven children from the problems in our marriage, but I knew I couldn't hide such pain from perceptive children. I cooked meals, cleaned, drove carpools to school, and then sobbed on the way home. I forced myself to clean my house, and then I would just lie down and cry because I hurt so much. Intense grief weighed on me every second. And my children sensed it.

At this point I was convinced that Steven could not help himself and I felt I must be there to save him. With determined self-sufficiency and a belief that God would help us, I began to learn about addiction and my husband's history with it. I found a therapist, I read the books, I frequently asked how he was doing, and even attended a twelve-step support group with him.

He didn't like the twelve-step group and didn't feel like he belonged there, but he agreed to attend therapy with me for a year. The method of therapy for him was, "Don't think about it anymore." After each session I would find myself needing validation and ask him, "Is this working for you? Are you doing better?" It was exhausting for both of us. After a year of therapy, he decided he was fine and sober and no longer needed any help. I chose to believe him, not knowing what else to do.

So on that beautiful fall morning in 2005 when I surrendered him to God, I believed with all my heart that I had done everything I could. I had encouraged him, loved him, helped him, and tried to guide him away from the destructive path he had been on for decades. I knew there was only one source of infinite power that could help him now. Steven had had his own surrender experience brought about by hitting rock bottom and began a process of doing whatever it took to overcome his shame, dishonesty, fear, lies, and immoral behavior. He realized he could not do it on his own.

He sat with each of our children and their spouses separately and told them his story. He pleaded for their forgiveness and committed to a mighty change of heart. In that painful setting, I began to see my husband as an honest, humble, and accountable man. This recognition gave me a small glimpse of what could be if he chose to consistently walk the path of recovery. He knew how to stop the behavior; he had stopped thousands of times. What he needed to learn was how to not start again.

I didn't know whether Steven could or would do what it would take. In his all-out effort, he found a qualified therapist and began to throw himself into the work of therapy. He found a good twelve-step group; one with men who had similar stories and long-term recovery. He chose to be mentored by one of them. He went weekly, sometimes more often, to a twelve-step meeting without being asked or reminded.

He also moved his things out to the camper that was in the

back of our property. This was his choice, a boundary he had set for himself. He knew he needed space and time to seriously look at himself and start the process of recovery. I also needed time and space to find some peace without him triggering me. I stood back for months and did not get emotionally involved. I waited to see what he would do. I was numb. I asked God every day when I could leave and continually got the answer that I should stay for the time being.

My instincts were to slow down and turn to God. Looking back at the trauma that this betrayal caused in my life, I see how important it was to take it easy, to learn to take care of myself, to meditate, pray, and look for God's hand in my life in simple ways.

Hesitantly, I joined Steven in therapy and began to learn that I could find a way beyond the betrayal. I learned that I would know the red flags of addict behavior without having to believe what my husband said. I learned that I would know I could trust God's inspiration speaking directly to me.

I did not understand the critical need for my recovery and healing until several years into the process of watching my husband work his own recovery. I found love and support from a caring church leader who was willing to hold my husband accountable for his behavior. I read, studied, and went to therapy, including group therapy, in order to understand the nature of pornography and sexual addiction. I learned to recognize addict behavior such as denial, justification, blame, victim, and shame in my husband. When I saw these behaviors, I held a boundary based on my need for safety and peace.

I learned I needed support from other women who knew the pain and wanted to make positive changes in their lives. My life has been filled with positive connections with women who are striving to be physically, emotionally, and spiritually healthy. I have found direction and a deeper connection with God through actively working the twelve steps. I am grateful to my sponsor, who has guided me through her strength, hope, and experience, to continue to work the steps, find safety, and be true to myself. I have deep appreciation for the many women I now rub shoulders with who work their own recovery in spite of broken marriages and difficult circumstances. Together we make a small but mighty army of courageous women who stand for truth and against evil.

It has been more than nine years since that life-changing experience for both of us. Our marriage that hung in the balance not only has endured but, through hard work, pain, and the grace of God, has flourished. One might ask, how do you work through that kind of pain and deceit? How do you truly move forward? The following section includes some of the most helpful ideas and tools that guided me on the rocky path of my own recovery.

1) Recovery is a process, and pain that leads to progress is part of the journey.

Recovery is a *process*; it is not an *event*. We are part of a quick-fix generation; we just want to get things done. We want a six-week program. This will not take six weeks! It will become a lifelong journey of constant learning. Recovery is not a short-term process, because recovery means continually cultivating a healthier lifestyle. Not only is the pain of recovery a process, it is transformative. We are being refined as God "makes our heart as gold."

God gives us opportunities in our lives that sometimes hurt abominably. Yet what he is doing is transforming us from average women to exceptional women. The process is not comfortable, but it is worth it.

None of us wants pain. Even worse than feeling our own pain is seeing our children or loved ones in pain. As mothers and as women, we do not like to see people hurt. Yet, as I look at my own life, I realize that my heavenly Father knows I'm going to experience pain—and he allows it to happen. He knows that pain and struggle will bring me closer to him in humility.

When my husband was arrested for soliciting a prostitute, my family was traumatized all over again. My children were furious and devastated, and I was in shock. My husband felt utterly humiliated. But it was the very torment he needed to interrupt his course in life. That experience was so traumatizing that he finally realized how out of control his life was. He now sees that torment, that interruption, as a gift from God. In retrospect, he contends that the arresting officers in their blue uniforms were actually angels who were sent to declare, "This is your opportunity."

How many of us as mothers and wives have the courage to allow our spouses or children to face the consequences of their own actions—and be blessed by the potential growth? What if I had stood in the way of that? What if I had minimized the effect his behavior had on our family by choosing to sweep everything under the rug? I would have swept away opportunity for growth.

When we look to the future, we may fear that we can't possibly overcome our most difficult challenges. But those challenges are exactly what we need. We should not opt out of such experiences in our lives; we should keep moving forward. And with God's loving care, he will get us through them—not just to survive but to triumph. We will find that we are more than we were when we began.

2) Setting boundaries—the most loving thing I can do.
God has set boundaries that help me feel safe and find peace in my life. Those boundaries are called commandments. I

know he has given those boundaries to me because he loves me. I, too, set boundaries because of my love for other people. That is why I say that setting and holding boundaries is the most loving thing I can do. I like the quote from psychologists Cloud and Townsend that says, "Go soft on the person and hard on the issue." Pornography violates Christian values such as faithfulness, honesty, holiness, loving God, and loving others. I must go hard on the issue of pornography, but I can still love my husband (though it may feel like "tough love").

Often when I feel the craziness come back into my life because I don't feel safe with my husband's behavior, I detach as a way to hold a boundary for safety.

Self-help author Melodie Beattie gives excellent advice on how and when to detach with love:

> When do we detach? When we are hooked into a reaction of anger, fear, guilt, or shame. When we get hooked into a power play, an attempt to control or force others to do something they don't want to do. When the way we're reacting isn't helping the other person or solving the problem.
>
> When the way we are reacting is hurting us. Often, it is time to detach when detachment appears to be the least likely, or possible, thing to do. (This is when a call to a sponsor is such a great blessing.) The first step toward detachment is understanding that reacting and controlling don't help. The next step is getting peaceful—getting centered and restoring our balance. Take a walk. Leave the room. Go to a meeting. Take a long, hot bath. Call a friend. Call on God. Breathe deeply. Find peace. From the place of peace and centering will emerge an answer, a solution.

3) Forgiveness is not the same as trust.

While my husband was learning to be honest every day in every way, I held back, not wanting to be vulnerable and run the risk of being wounded again. However, I knew that forgiveness was critical for my inner peace. I determined to open a spot in my heart to be able to forgive. That forgiveness process was going to be something I worked out between God and myself. As I have prayed to forgive, that spot in my heart has filled with a wonderful gift that I know is between God and me.

Trust, on the other hand, when broken, must be rebuilt one day at a time. My husband is working each day to earn my trust. I also am working each day to trust and be vulnerable. I have also worked at being honest at expressing my feelings and needs. My husband and I use a vowel check-in every night in our effort for continued daily honesty.

A—Abstinence (For example: my husband's abstinence is from lust and mine is from fear)

E—Exercise

I—Something I did for self-care

O—Some service I gave to others

U—Unexpressed emotion

Y—Yay for the day (the best thing that happened today or for which I am especially grateful)

4) The miracle of surrender. Steps 1, 2, and 3 in practice.

The Serenity Prayer guides me each day. There is so much I cannot control. I can wear myself out emotionally and even physically trying to change other people and circumstances. So, I recognize the most important part of my recovery is surrendering my will to God. He knows me, he loves me, and he will take my burdens. I need to let him.

Steps 1, 2, and 3 of the twelve-step program remind me that my life is unmanageable in many ways, that God can bring me back to serenity, and that I must let him as I give my will to his. This is not easy for me, and I work my surrender process on my knees, on the phone, and in the box. Whenever I lose my serenity about anything, I go to my knees in prayer and ask God to take the thing that is bothering me. Then I get up and phone my sponsor. If she doesn't answer, I leave a message expressing my surrender. Then I write on a small piece of paper the burden I would like God to take from me, fold it up, and put it in what I call my surrender box. This process works. Especially if I do it multiple times if the same concern keeps coming back.

The willingness to be vulnerable and surrender my life to God is the way to my empowerment and serenity. This, the greatest paradox of recovery, raises the question, "How can it be?"

The answer lies in the courage to change the things I can—the courage to do something about *me*.

After three years of working recovery one day at a time, my husband and I recognized that there was a great need for thousands of individuals, couples, and families to have hope and a pathway to recovery from the effects of pornography and sexual addiction. Too many families were being broken apart and devastated by this issue. With a lot of prayer and faith, we began a nonprofit foundation called SA Lifeline Foundation. Our website, books, and manuals offer education and information regarding this issue.

Now, six years later, thousands of people have found information, and most of all hope, for recovery based on the work of the foundation. We recently started our own gender-specific twelve-step groups that offer safety and emphasize God at the center of recovery. These groups recognize the critical nature of doing all that it takes to find long-term healing for individuals and families. These groups are helping save marriages and families.

My husband and I are committed to our own recovery and also to the recovery of our marriage. Working one day at a time blesses our lives, the lives of our children, their spouses, and our eighteen grandchildren. We are a family that has been blessed by the grace of God.

Appendix

The following Scripture verses have been carefully selected by Cameron and me for your meditation. They focus on the comfort, strength, and restoration God our Father wants to give you. Our suggestion is that you 1) offer a prayer before reading each passage from Scripture, 2) meditate slowly upon the words of one particular verse, and then 3) offer a prayer of thanksgiving after reading the passage for what you have received from the verse.

Prayer Before Reading Scripture

Lord, inspire me to read your Scripture and to meditate upon it day and night. I beg you to give me real understanding of what I need, that I, in turn, may put its precepts into practice. Yet, I know that understanding and good intentions are worthless, unless rooted in your graceful love. So I ask that the words of Scripture may also be not just signs on a page, but channels of grace into my heart. Amen.

Prayer After Reading Scripture

God of holiness, whose promises stand through all generations, fulfill the longings of a humanity weighed down by confusion and burdened with fear. Raise up our heads and strengthen our hearts, that we may proclaim to all people the

Good News of your presence in our midst. May we delight to share with them your peace, which surpasses all understanding.

We ask this through our Lord Jesus Christ, your Son, who lives and reigns with you in the unity of the Holy Spirit, one God forever and ever. Amen

"The Lord is my shepherd, I shall not want; he makes me lie down in green pastures. He leads me beside still waters; he restores my soul." —Psalm 23:1-3

"When Jesus saw him and knew that he had been lying there a long time, he said to him, "Do you want to be healed?" —John 5:6

"And after you have suffered a little while, the God of all grace, who has called you to his eternal glory in Christ, will himself restore, establish, and strengthen you. To him be the dominion forever and ever. Amen." —1 Peter 5:10-11

"God did not give us a spirit of timidity but a spirit of power and love and self-control." —2 Timothy 1:7

"May you be strengthened with all power, according to his glorious might, for all endurance and patience with joy, giving thanks to the Father, who has qualified us to share in the inheritance of the saints in light." —Colossians 1:11-12

"Cast all your anxieties on him, for he cares about you." —1 Peter 5:7

"Blessed be the God and Father of our Lord Jesus Christ, the Father of mercies and God of all comfort, who comforts us in all our affliction, so that we may be able to comfort those who are in any affliction, with the comfort with which we ourselves are comforted by God. For as we share abundantly in Christ's sufferings, so through Christ we share abundantly in comfort too." —2 Corinthians 1:3-5

"O afflicted one, storm-tossed, and not comforted, behold, I will set your stones in antimony, and lay your foundations with sapphires. I will make your pinnacles of agate, your gates of carbuncles, and all your wall of precious stones. . . . In righteousness you shall be established; you shall be far from oppression, for you shall not fear; and from terror, for it shall not come near you. —Isaiah 54:11-12;14

"Come to me, all who labor and are heavy laden, and I will give you rest. Take my yoke upon you, and learn from me; for I am gentle and lowly in heart, and you will find rest for your souls. For my yoke is easy, and my burden is light." —Matthew 11:28-30

"Truly, truly, I say to you, you will weep and lament, but the world will rejoice; you will be sorrowful, but your sorrow will turn into joy. . . . So you have sorrow now, but I will see you again and your hearts will rejoice, and no one will take your joy from you." —John 16:20, 22

"We know that in everything God works for good with those who love him, who are called according to his purpose." —Romans 8:28

"For I know the plans I have for you, says the Lord, plans for welfare and not for evil, to give you a future and a hope. Then you will call upon me and come and pray to me, and I will hear you. You will seek me and find me; when you seek me with all your heart." —Jeremiah 29:11-13

"Peace I leave with you; my peace I give to you; not as the world gives do I give to you. Let not your hearts be troubled, neither let them be afraid." —John 14:27

"When the righteous cry for help, the Lord hears, and delivers them out of all their troubles. The Lord is near to the broken-hearted, and saves the crushed in spirit." —Psalm 34:17-18

"I heard a loud voice from the throne saying, "Behold, the dwelling of God is with men. He will dwell with them, and they shall be his people, and God himself will be with them; he will wipe away every tear from their eyes, and death shall be no more, neither shall there be mourning nor crying nor pain any more, for the former things have passed away." —Revelation 21:3-4

I have said this to you, that in me you may have peace. In the world you have tribulation; but be of good cheer, I have overcome the world." —John 16:33

"So we do not lose heart. Though our outer nature is wasting away, our inner nature is being renewed every day. For this slight momentary affliction is preparing for us an eternal weight of glory beyond all comparison, because we look not to the things that are seen but to the things that are unseen; for the things that are seen are transient, but the things that are unseen are eternal." —2 Corinthians 4:16-18

"Say to those who are of a fearful heart, "Be strong, fear not! Behold, your God will come with vengeance, with the recompense of God. He will come and save you." —Isaiah 35:4

"Therefore all who devour you shall be devoured, and all your foes, every one of them, shall go into captivity; those who despoil you shall become a spoil, and all who prey on you I will make a prey. For I will restore health to you, and your wounds I will heal, says the Lord." —Jeremiah 30:16-17

"Behold, I make all things new." —Revelation 21:5

"Rejoice in the Lord always; again I will say, Rejoice. Let all men know your forbearance. The Lord is at hand. Have no anxiety about anything, but in everything by prayer and supplication with thanksgiving let your requests be made known to God. And the peace of God, which passes all understanding, will keep your hearts and your minds in Christ Jesus." —Philippians 4:4-8

"Restore to me the joy of thy salvation, and uphold me with a willing spirit." —Psalm 51

"God is our refuge and strength, a very present help in trouble. Therefore we will not fear though the earth should change, though the mountains shake in the heart of the sea; though its waters roar and foam, though the mountains tremble with its tumult." —Psalm 46:1-3

"Behold, I am doing a new thing; now it springs forth, do you not perceive it? I will make a way in the wilderness and rivers in the desert." —Isaiah 43:19

"A new heart I will give you, and a new spirit I will put within you; and I will take out of your flesh the heart of stone and give you a heart of flesh." —Ezekiel 36:26

Contributors

Matt Fradd is the executive director of *The Porn Effect*, a website dedicated to helping men and women break free from pornography. He is the editor of *Delivered: True Stories of Men and Women who Turned From Porn to Purity* and co-author of *Victory: A Strategic Battle Plan for Freedom in the Struggle Against Pornography*. Matt speaks to tens of thousands of people every year on the dangers of pornography and how to be free from it. He lives in Georgia with his wife Cameron and their four children.

Cameron Fradd is passionate about helping women discover their identity as beloved daughters of God, and encouraging them to live out that identity. She spends most of her time raising four energetic and beautiful children in Georgia, where she lives with a husband she loves and a cat she tolerates. You can follow her on Twitter, @CameronFradd.

Elisa spends her time raising and schooling her five children. She is happily married to her best friend Chester. She loves to help others find a deeper relationship with Christ by being honest and transparent. In any "free time" she has, Elisa paints and explores with her family. Follow her on Instagram, @ejmac.

Christina is a member of a twelve-step program that helps the friends and relatives of people affected by sex addiction. She has found recovery through working the twelve steps and turning her life over to the care of God. She gives back what has been given to her by sponsoring and sharing her story with others. Christina is also an active member of a Catholic parish where she teaches faith formation. She lives in the Pacific Northwest with her husband.

Mimi and Matt live in the Washington, D.C metro area with their beautiful baby daughter. Mimi is a math teacher and Matt serves as a men's campus minister at a local state university. Together they run the site Catholicfriedrice.com, which covers a variety of Catholic topics including Matt's porn recovery.

Rachel and John live in Kansas City. In December 2014, they founded King David's Rock, a ministry that stresses prevention and masculinity as important tools to fight the harmful effects of internet pornography. You can reach Rachel at info@kingdavidsrock.org.

Polly is the spokeswoman for bloomforwomen.com, She uses her personal experiences as the wife of a sex addict to educate and empower women to find personal peace. Her goal is to bring awkward subjects to light without fear or shame and to help people connect with their loved ones. She and her husband have three adorable children. To contact Polly, email polly@bloomforwomen.com.

Anne lives in southeastern Michigan with her husband Paul. She is passionate about encouraging other wives to heal through this journey, while finding joy and beauty in life. Each day is another opportunity to grow in serenity and trust God's plan. You can contact her at choosejoy.belove@gmail.com.

Amy is wife to Jesse and homeschooling mother of twelve children on earth and nine in heaven. She lives with her family in the wonderful state of Michigan. You can follow her family's ups and downs at www.ekblad9.blogspot.com.

Ana is a wife, mother, and registered nurse with a passion to tell her personal stories in the hopes of inspiring others. Born in a small Midwest farming town, Ana was raised as a cradle Catholic but did not begin to deeply explore her faith until her college years. In 2015, Ana and her husband developed www.freedandrestored.com as a resource to share their story and encourage anyone affected by pornography addiction. Ana lives in Michigan with her husband Ryan and their three children.

Maya is a college student studying psychology. She is dedicated to living out her Catholic faith, and serving as a youth leader, while also remaining open to God's will along the way. She resides in California.

Rhyll is the co-founder, vice-president, and executive director of SA Lifeline Foundation. The foundation is active in providing information and education to those impacted by pornography and sexual addiction. She is a music teacher, and a student at Brigham Young University studying Marriage and Family Relations. She has interned in the area of sexual addiction recovery and has been a speaker at numerous women's conferences. She and her husband Steve have four sons, three daughters and fourteen grandchildren. You can reach Rhyll at rhyll@salifeline.org.

Matt Fradd experienced a profound conversion to Jesus Christ in the year 2000 and afterward committed himself to inviting others to know Jesus Christ and the Church Christ founded.

Passionate about helping others affected by porn and pornography addiction, Matt now speaks to tens of thousands of people every year about the peace and healing that comes through Jesus Christ.

Matt is the executive director of integrityrestored.com and theporneffect.com.

To schedule Matt to speak at your next event, visit:

integrityrestored.com/conferences

INTEGRITY RESTORED™

Our mission at Integrity Restored is to restore the integrity of individuals, spouses, and families that have been affected by pornography and pornography addiction.

Integrity Restored provides education, encouragement, and resources to break free from pornography, heal relationships, and to assist parents in preventing and responding to pornography exposure which is so devastating in the lives of our children.

We also hope to be a resource that assists clergy in assisting families at the parish level, so that the domestic church truly becomes what it is, the human space in which we encounter Christ.

Visit us at - integrityrestored.com

Integrity Restored is a ministry of Stewardship: A Mission of Faith, a 501(c)(3) non-profit organization.